The Quilter's Negative Space Handbook

Step-by-Step Design Instruction
and 8 Modern Projects

Sylvia Schaefer

stashBOOKS®
an imprint of C&T Publishing

Publisher: Amy Marson

Creative Director: Gailen Runge

Acquisitions Editor: Roxane Cerda

Managing Editor: Liz Aneloski

Editor: Christine Doyle

Technical Editor: Nan Powell

Cover/Book Designer: April Mostek

Production Coordinator: Zinnia Heinzmann

Production Editor: Alice Mace Nakanishi

Illustrator: Aliza Shalit

Photo Assistants: Rachel Holmes and Mai Yong Vang

Style photography by Kelly Burgoyne and quilt and instructional photography by Mai Yong Vang of C&T Publishing, Inc., unless otherwise noted

Library of Congress Cataloging-in-Publication Data

Names: Schaefer, Sylvia, 1979- author.

Title: The quilter's negative space handbook : step-by-step design instruction and 8 modern projects / Sylvia Schaefer.

Description: Lafayette, CA : C&T Publishing, Inc., 2019.

Identifiers: LCCN 2018018975 | ISBN 9781617456794 (soft cover)

Subjects: LCSH: Patchwork--Patterns. | Quilting--Patterns.

Classification: LCC TT835 .S2847 2019 | DDC 746.46/041--dc23

LC record available at https://lccn.loc.gov/2018018975

Printed in China

10 9 8 7 6 5 4 3 2 1

Dedication

To my husband, Adrian, who carries my bolts of fabric and doesn't judge the size of my stash.

Acknowledgments

Special thanks to my family for their love and support of all my quilting endeavors: my husband, Adrian, and my mother, Karin. Thank you to the Cotton Patch Quilters of Athens, Georgia, whose questions about modern quilting and negative space sparked the ideas in this book, and to the Athens modern quilting group for their tireless cheerleading along every step of my journey, especially Marybeth Tawfik.

Thanks to Robert Kaufman for providing Kona Cottons for *Northern Lights* and to Cassandra Ireland Beaver for quilting it. Thanks to Frances Arnold for allowing me to include a photo of her mother's beautiful quilt. Last but certainly not least, I am so grateful to the entire C&T team for giving me the opportunity to share my ideas and for making this book a reality!

Contents

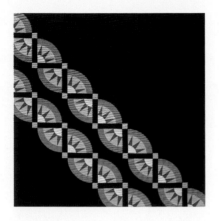

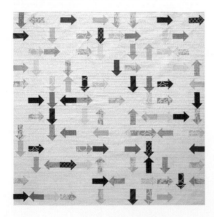

 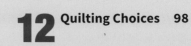

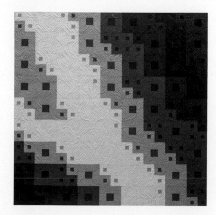
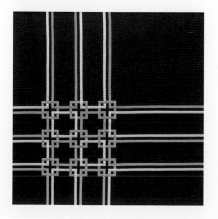

Preface

After giving a presentation on modern quilting to my local traditional quilt guild, the quilters were particularly intrigued by the idea of negative space. Could I come up with another program for them focusing on this aspect of modern quilting?

While thinking about what I could tell them that would actually be useful, I realized that many members were what I like to call "modern-curious": appreciative of the modern quilting aesthetic but from a traditional quilting background and a little intimidated by the idea of trying to design something with a lot of negative space. What they needed were concrete steps to take something they were familiar with—a traditional block or existing quilt—and modify it, step by step, to include negative space.

I suspect that my friends in Georgia are not the only ones who aspire to design their own modern quilts but don't know where to begin, so I would like to share these ideas with you, too. I'll take traditional blocks or quilt patterns and go through the design process step by step. Each chapter will focus on particular concepts to apply to your design, such as removing elements or disintegration (my personal favorite!). You'll also find chapters on fabric, quilting choices, and more to help you turn your idea into a reality.

I used to get into creative slumps where I'd sit in my sewing room wanting to sew but unable to decide what to make next. Ever since I came up with the ideas in this book, I've had a vast backlog of project ideas. I hope that you, too, will find a flood of inspiration in these pages. I can't wait to see what amazing designs you come up with, so let's get started!

Introduction

What Is Negative Space?

If you have picked up this book, you probably already have a good idea of what negative space is, but it's always good to start with a definition. In art, *negative space* is defined simply as the space surrounding or in between the subject or subjects of the artwork, and it's every bit as important as the positive space, which is occupied by the subject. The point of negative space is to give the eye a place to rest, but it should also help the eye move across the piece and draw attention to the main subject.

Shoes, painting by Vincent van Gogh, 1888

The bricks that the shoes rest on are the negative space. There is plenty of detail in the bricks, yet they are clearly not the focus of the painting.

Still Life with Apples and a Pot of Primroses, painting by Paul Cézanne, ca. 1890

The walls are part of the negative space; the tablecloth is too, since it fills the space between the real subjects of the painting, the apples.

When it comes to quilts, it's easiest to think of negative space as the background of your quilt.
This could be the background of the quilt as a whole or just the background within individual blocks. Many beloved traditional quilt designs incorporate negative space, often within a block.

Modern art and design, where negative space is also sometimes referred to as *white space*, place a particular emphasis on minimalism, and extended areas of negative space are common. Modern quilts, too, often have expansive negative space. While definitions of modern quilting range all over the place, a quilt with extensive negative space, particularly if that negative space is asymmetrically arranged, tends to read as modern.

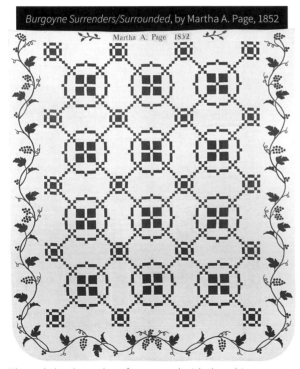

Burgoyne Surrenders/Surrounded, by Martha A. Page, 1852

The red clearly reads as foreground with the white as background or negative space.

Boston Commons, by Lois Swinson, ca. 1976

This is a traditional pattern, but it incorporates large areas of white negative space across the whole quilt.

Photo (*left*): Public domain, Creative Commons Zero (CC0) from The Metropolitan Museum of Art

How to Use This Book

The goal of this book is to give you the tools to design your own modern quilts that incorporate negative space. You need a starting point, though, and if you've never tried designing your own quilt before, you might be wondering where to find that first spark.

Here, you will use two possible starting points.

 **The first option is starting with a traditional quilt, in which you can change the colors or remove elements to create negative space** (Chapter 2). This is the best place to start if you are completely new to modern quilting.

 **The other option is to start with a traditional quilt block and develop it into a modern quilt by surrounding it with negative space.** This might seem a little more daunting at first, but you will explore a number of different ideas for arranging or modifying your chosen block (Chapters 3 to 9), and I hope you will find a world of new options opening up to you.

Of course, the design of your quilt is only the beginning. You also need to choose fabrics, figure out how to make the quilt, and eventually, how to quilt it. An overview of some of your options is included (Chapters 10 to 12).

1

Getting Started

To actually design a quilt using the concepts in this book, you need to find some blocks or patterns to start with. You also need a way to visualize your design as you refine it. Fortunately, you have a lot of choices for both.

Finding Quilt Blocks and Patterns

The negative space exists to enhance the main subject of your quilt: the piecing. Since this book focuses on creating modern quilts from traditional patterns, you will usually want to start your quilt design by choosing a quilt block. If you have a favorite block, that would be a good choice when starting your first foray into the block-based design ideas. You will find yourself more inspired when working with something you love.

To find new favorites, collections of quilt blocks are always good investments. An encyclopedia of quilt blocks (see Resources, page 110) is an excellent and inspiring reference no matter what type of quilting you are most interested in. Sampler quilt patterns, particularly those that include a large number of blocks, are also good sources of inspiration. There are many such patterns available, such as the Dear Jane quilts based on a 225-block quilt made by Jane A. Stickle in 1863, as well as many modern options.

And, of course, this being the twenty-first century, there's the internet. A search for "quilt blocks" (or refine it if you know what you're looking for) will keep you clicking on tutorials long past bedtime.

Tools for Designing

You've got a quilt block and you've got some ideas on how to turn it into an amazing quilt. How do you start visualizing what your finished quilt might look like?

I like to use electronic tools to design quilts, as I find this allows me the greatest ease in testing color schemes and playing with the size and placement of my blocks. There is a variety of dedicated quilt design software now available. I primarily use Electric Quilt, but there are others, including web-based programs and even apps for your smartphone or tablet. Microsoft Word and PowerPoint are also workable design tools, if purchasing a specialized software package is not an option.

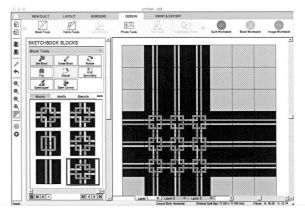

Designing a quilt using Electric Quilt 8 software

While quilt design software is plenty for most quilts, I find it helpful in certain cases to supplement this with a more general graphic design program that will allow me to manipulate individual elements of a block. I use Adobe Illustrator; Inkscape is a free alternative. These software programs have a steeper learning curve, but it can be useful to have them in your toolbox for some of the designs that move out of a traditional block format, such as you will find when using the disintegration technique (page 58), and some designers prefer to do all their work in them.

If designing on the computer isn't your cup of tea, graph paper is a tried-and-true alternative. Combine it with colored pencils to explore your color and design options. It is often helpful to be able to move blocks around; draw an outline of your block and then make photocopies to color in, cut out, and rearrange.

Designing a quilt using paper and colored pencils

Design
Techniques

Each of the following chapters focuses on a particular concept for organizing your negative space. While some are better suited to blocks with particular characteristics, most blocks can work with several different concepts; the only limit is your imagination. Keep an open mind, and don't ever be afraid to experiment!

2

Removing Elements

If you admire quilts with extensive negative space, but have never designed such a quilt, it can be hard to know where to start. Faced with a blank canvas, what should you add and where? It can all be very overwhelming, so try starting, instead, with a "traditional" quilt: blocks laid out in rows, maybe with sashings and a border. You probably have many patterns like this in your collection. Instead of having to add elements to create an interesting quilt design with negative space, you can do something far easier—start removing things!

Removing Elements by Changing Colors

The simplest method of "removing things" actually involves removing nothing at all, just rethinking your fabric choices.

Take a fairly traditional-looking sampler quilt like this one.

What if you used more subdued fabric choices for half your blocks, in order to allow the eye to focus on just a few rows of blocks?

NOTE | *For more ideas on setting blocks in rows, see Chapter 5 (page 42).*

Notice that by using gray tones in the stars, you have allowed the pieced blocks to remain recognizable, but they fade into the negative space. The border looks odd in this design, so you could change that to the background fabric as well to provide your blocks some breathing room and just frame the design with your binding.

Removing Elements Altogether

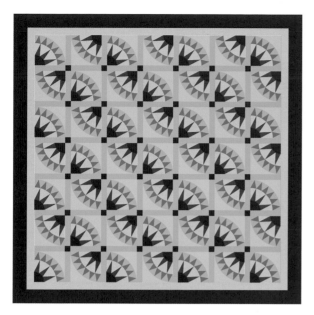

If you are ready to think about removing elements altogether, take a look at this traditional quilt layout featuring New York Beauty blocks. The first step is to identify the background color or fabric.

Although it's not the color occupying the most extensive area, the light blue surrounding the spiked arcs of the blocks looks like the background of the blocks. How can you make it more prominent?

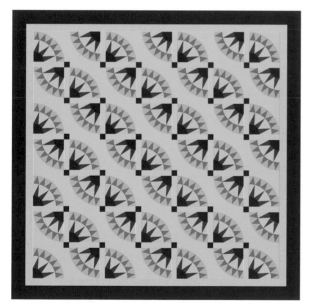

The first thing you might do is recolor the sashing to light blue. This is a very different quilt design already! Notice how, just by recoloring that one element, you have opened up the quilt design and there is now interesting diagonal motion.

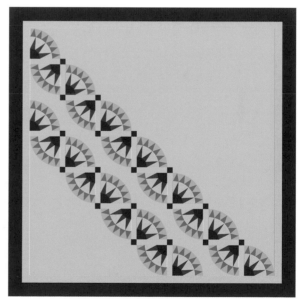

To emphasize this diagonal motion further, you could keep only a few of the diagonal lines you have created. Just like that, you have an interesting quilt with a lot of negative space.

The borders hem in the diagonal movement in the quilt, so try dropping them altogether.

NOTE | *Now is a good time to play around with colors. Flip to Northern Lights (page 19) to find this pattern in a different color scheme.*

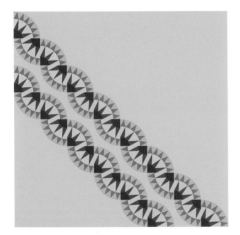

You could also try completely removing the sashing, but this doesn't look as good. Don't hesitate to take a step backward in your design process and put elements back in if they added to the design!

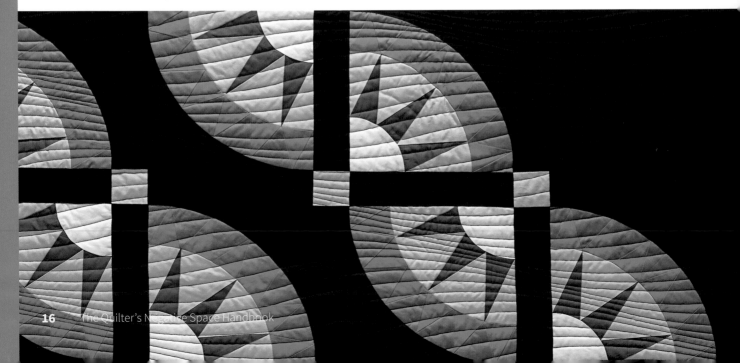

Varying Block Sizes

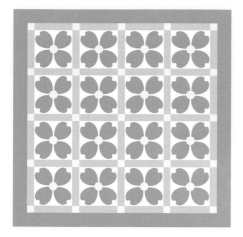

Consider another traditional layout, such as this one, an appliqué quilt.

Again, you need to identify the existing background. In this case, it's obvious: the white that the flowers are appliquéd onto. As with the last example, you could recolor all of the sashing and the borders to that white.

There is a lot more negative space now, but what happens if you remove some of the flowers? You don't necessarily have to remove them in rows; you could do so randomly.

The idea wasn't bad, but you don't want the viewer to think you got bored and ran out of steam making blocks (even if that's what happened)! One way to make this design decision look deliberate, but keep some of those open spaces, is to vary the block size.

The blocks are still laid out in a grid, making the quilt easy to piece. Of course, you could include more than two sizes of blocks. Play around to see what looks best to you!

Adjusting Backgrounds

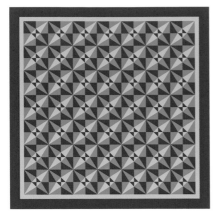

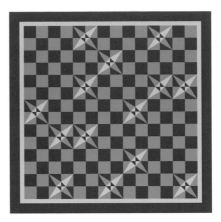

This busy quilt features the Crossed Canoes block. What is the background here? If you think of the actual "canoes" as the main element, it becomes clear that they are set against a checkerboard.

Try removing some blocks as you did in the previous example, leaving just background. The background dominates this quilt design and detracts from the crossed canoes that you are trying to draw attention to.

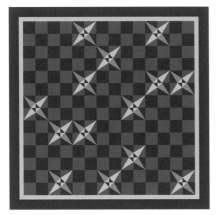

Instead of replacing the checkerboard with a solid, though, you could just change the green to another shade of blue in order to tone down the checkerboard effect and still keep an interesting texture in the background.

This is a good illustration of the fact that negative space doesn't have to mean a sea of solid fabric. However, you do need to make sure that it doesn't detract from the star (no pun intended) of your design. As a final move, you can play with the colors to increase contrast, and you can also adjust border widths.

TIP

Try arranging the stars in the shape of your favorite constellation!

Now, it's your turn to look through your stash of patterns for quilts just waiting for a modern twist!

Northern Lights

By removing all but a couple diagonal lines of blocks from a traditional layout of New York Beauty blocks, the wavy movement in them is brought out. Choose greens and aqua against a rich bluish-purple night sky to create a quilt reminiscent of the aurora borealis.

Finished block:
9″ × 9″

Finished quilt:
75½″ × 75½″

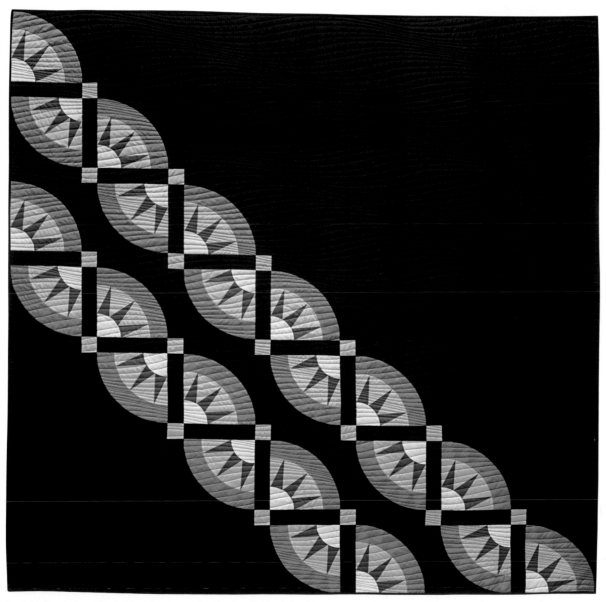

Designed and pieced by Sylvia Schaefer, quilted by Cassandra Ireland Beaver, 2017

Materials

Dark purple solid:
5¼ yards for background

Pale green solid:
⅜ yard for blocks

Light green solid:
1½ yards for blocks and
sashing cornerstones

Medium green solid:
¾ yard for blocks

Dark green solid:
¾ yard for blocks

Aqua solid:
1¼ yards for blocks

Batting: 83˝ × 83˝

Backing: 4⅝ yards

Binding: ⅝ yards

Cutting

Purple

- Cut 10 strips 2½˝ × width of fabric; subcut into 39 strips 9½˝ × 2½˝ for sashing.

- Cut 22 background arcs, using patterns D1 and D2 (page 25) for background. Follow the directions to copy patterns D1 and D2 and tape together along the dotted lines.

- Cut background strips for the negative space. (For the best way to cut the background pieces, see the cutting diagram, below.)

1 strip 64½˝ × 11½˝	1 strip 31½˝ × 11½˝	1 square 11½˝ × 11½˝
1 strip 53½˝ × 11½˝	1 strip 22½˝ × 11½˝	1 strip 9½˝ × 11½˝
1 strip 42½˝ × 11½˝	1 strip 20½˝ × 11½˝	1 strip 33½˝ × 9½˝

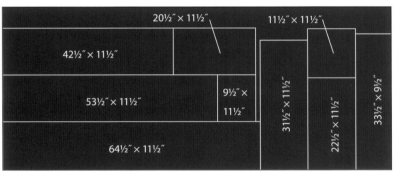

Cutting diagram for background strips

Light green

- Cut 2 strips 2½˝ × width of fabric; subcut into 18 squares 2½˝ × 2½˝ for sashing cornerstones. Set aside the rest for paper piecing.

Solid fabrics

- To cut the pieces for paper piecing the blocks, refer to Cutting Fabrics for Paper Piecing (page 103).

Block Assembly

1 Make 22 copies of the paper-piecing patterns A, B, C1, and C2 (pages 23–25). Follow the directions to copy patterns C1 and C2 and tape together along the dotted lines.

2 Cut 22 A units from pale green solid using pattern A.

3 Paper piece arcs B and C; see Piecing Segments (page 105). Make sure to reduce your stitch length to 1–1.5 mm so that the seams will not unravel when piecing the finished arcs together using curved seams. Use light green solid and dark green solid for arc B; use medium green solid and aqua solid for arc C.

4 Remove the papers.

5 See Curved Piecing (page 108) to join arc unit A to B and unit C to D, then join the halves together, pressing as indicated by the arrows. **Fig. A**

Quilt Construction

1 Sew sashing strips to the right side of all but one of the blocks. Press toward sashing. Assemble the sashed blocks. **Fig. B**

2 Sew a cornerstone square to 18 of the sashing strips, then assemble in strips. **Fig. C**

3 Assemble the rows by adding the sashing strips to the bottom of all sets of blocks except the set without the right-hand sashing.

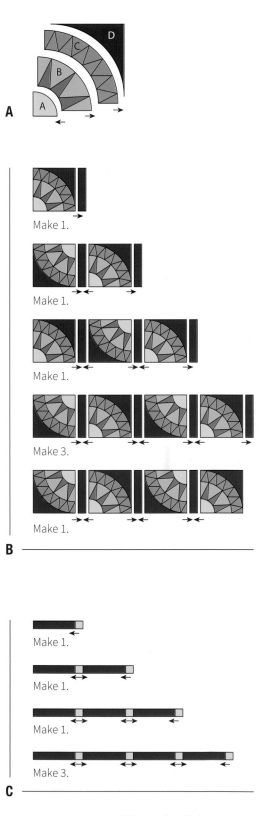

A

Make 1.

Make 1.

Make 1.

Make 3.

Make 1.

B

Make 1.

Make 1.

Make 1.

Make 3.

C

4 Sew the solid strips to the block units as follows:

- Sew the 64½″ × 11½″ strip to the right side of the single block.

- Sew the 53½″ × 11½″ strip to the right side of the 2-block unit.

- Sew the 42½″ × 11½″ strip to the right side of the 3-block unit.

- Sew the 31½″ × 11½″ to the right side of a 4-block unit with bottom sashing.

- Sew the 11½″ × 11½″ square to the left side of a 4-block unit with bottom sashing. Sew the 20½″ × 11½″ strip to the right side of that unit.

- Sew the 22½″ × 11½″ strip to the left side of a 4-block unit with bottom sashing. Sew the 9½″ × 11½″ strip to the right side of that unit.

- Sew the 33½″ × 9½″ strip to the left side of the 4-block unit without bottom sashing.

5 Sew the rows together, always pressing toward the sashing.

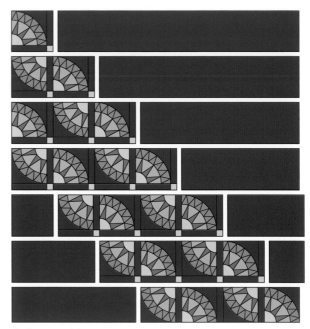

Quilt assembly

Finishing

Layer, quilt, and bind as desired.

The sample was quilted with an allover wavy pattern that is reminiscent of the undulating Northern Lights.

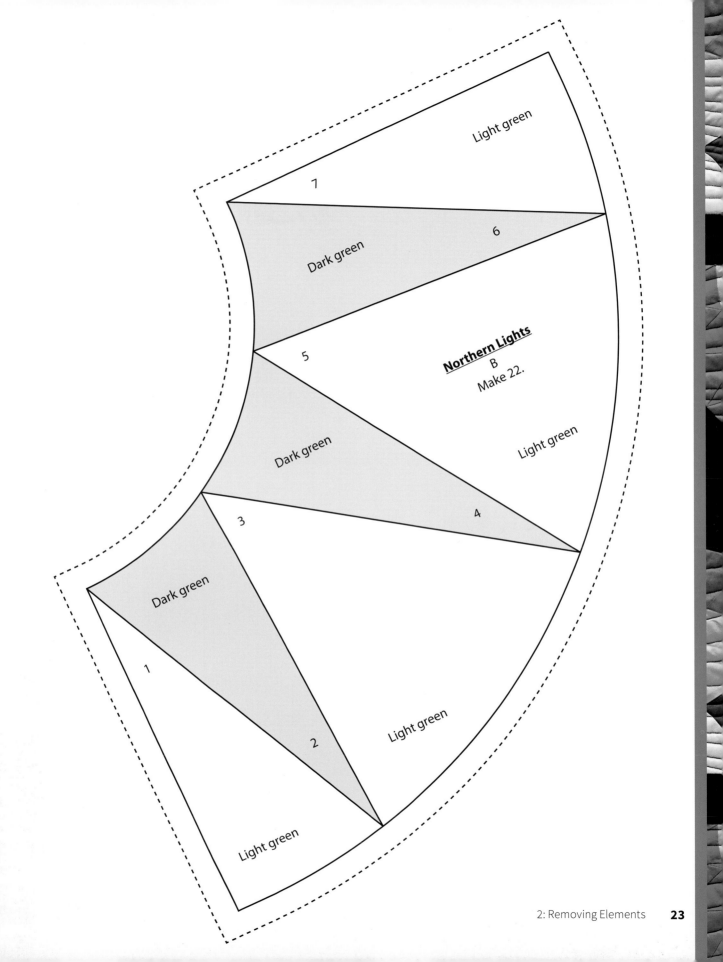

Light green

7

Dark green

6

Northern Lights
B
Make 22.

5

Dark green

Light green

4

3

Dark green

1

Light green

2

Light green

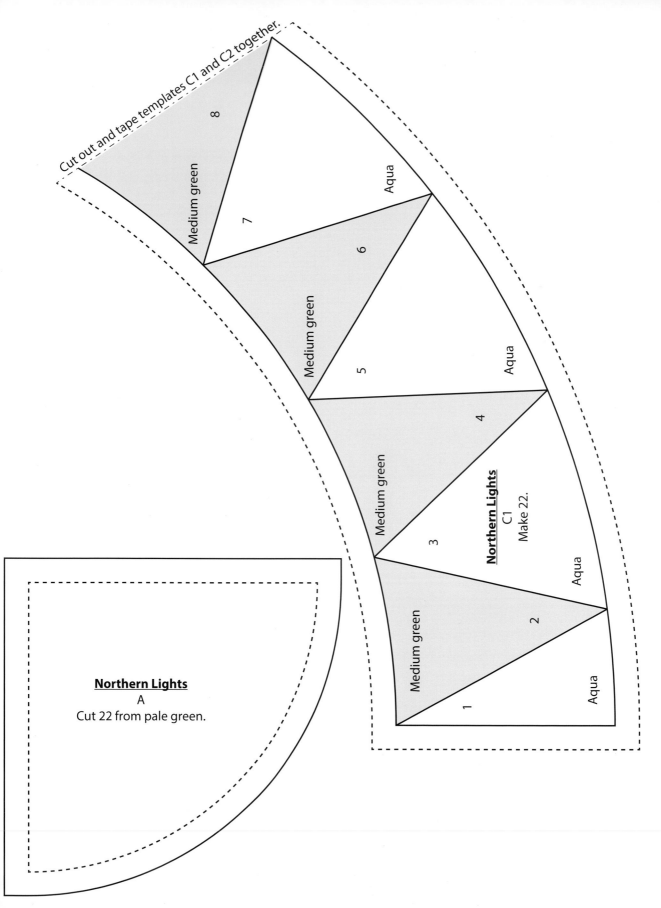

Cut out and tape templates C1 and C2 together.

8

Medium green

7

Aqua

6

Medium green

5

Aqua

Medium green

4

Northern Lights
C1
Make 22.

3

Aqua

Medium green

2

1

Aqua

Northern Lights
A
Cut 22 from pale green.

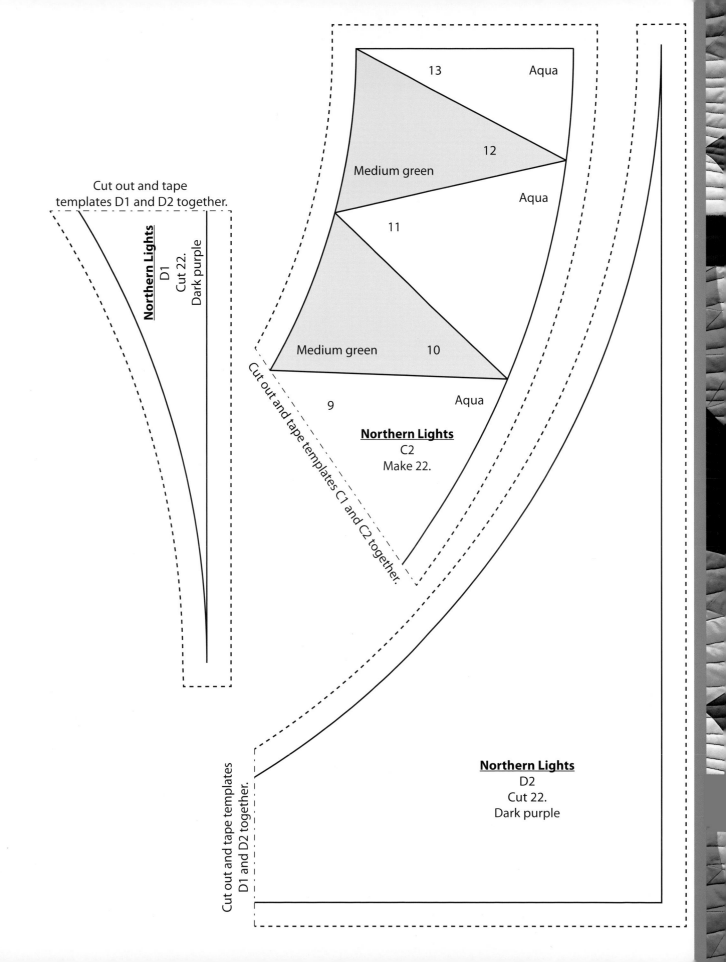

Cut out and tape
templates D1 and D2 together.

Northern Lights
D1
Cut 22.
Dark purple

13   Aqua

12

Medium green   Aqua

11

Medium green   10

Aqua

9

Cut out and tape templates C1 and C2 together.

Northern Lights
C2
Make 22.

Cut out and tape templates
D1 and D2 together.

Northern Lights
D2
Cut 22.
Dark purple

3

Standing Alone

If you are beginning your design process with a quilt block, the simplest way of incorporating negative space into the quilt is by letting the block speak for itself. This works best for relatively complex blocks, such as Lone Star or Mariner's Compass blocks that have sufficient interest to stand on their own. (For a discussion of ideas for simpler blocks, see Chapter 4, page 34.)

Deciding Whether to Add Anything

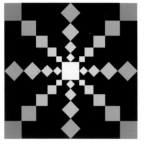

Because many traditional quilt blocks have a clearly defined background built in, you may from time to time find a traditional block, such as this Lightning block, that needs nothing further to stand on its own as a quilt.

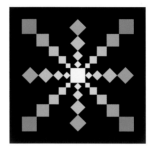

There is plenty of negative space (the black background) in this block, and any addition of borders would dilute the feeling of outward motion.

Adding Breathing Space

More often, though, a complex block benefits from some breathing space. Consider how the look of this Mariner's Compass is improved when surrounded by a wide border in the background color.

Setting the block in the quilt's center is not your only option, however. Placing it in a corner can create an interesting effect as well and consolidates the negative space.

Setting at an Angle

This is an example of a feathered star, a variation on a Lone Star block. You could start by placing this block in the corner of the quilt as in the previous example.

It's always a good idea to think about how your quilt design is creating movement. Placing a block at a slight angle can help create a sense of motion.

This would not have worked as well with the Mariner's Compass in the previous example, because rotation would simply have moved a different point into the upright position. With this eight-pointed star, however, you can choose an angle that makes the slight rotation appear intentional without moving the block to a fully on-point setting. Typically, about a 15° rotation is a good place to start.

NOTE | *For information on how to calculate and cut setting triangles for rotating a block, see Chapter 11 (page 92).*

To further add to the rotated and off-center effect, you can place the block partially off the edge of the quilt. To do this, you will cut off part of the block—this is definitely a little nerve-wracking, but the results are worth it!

You'll find the pattern for the quilt (far left) at the end of this chapter (*Icy Feathered Star*, page 28), but if you prefer the second design, simply cut off more of your star and add wider borders on the top and right-hand side.

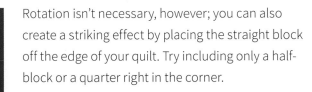

Rotation isn't necessary, however; you can also create a striking effect by placing the straight block off the edge of your quilt. Try including only a half-block or a quarter right in the corner.

Icy Feathered Star

The very traditional feathered star pattern gets a modern update by setting it at a jaunty angle and adding negative space on the sides. Finishing the quilt with a facing instead of binding keeps the motion from stopping at the edge of the quilt.

Finished block:
27″ × 27″

Finished quilt:
33″ × 39″

Made by Sylvia Schaefer, 2017

Materials

Light aqua solid:
1¾ yards for background

Assorted aqua prints:

Fabrics 1–5: ¼ yard for center lone star

Fabric 6: ½ yard for star's outer feathered edge

Batting: 41″ × 48″

Backing: 1½ yards

Facing: ⅓ yard

Cutting

Aqua fabric 1

- Cut 1 strip 1¾″ × width of fabric.

Aqua fabric 2

- Cut 2 strips 1¾″ × width of fabric.

Aqua fabric 3

- Cut 3 strips 1¾″ × width of fabric.

Aqua fabric 4

- Cut 2 strips 1¾″ × width of fabric.

Aqua fabric 5

- Cut 1 strip 1¾″ × width of fabric.

Aqua fabric 6

- To precut fabrics for paper piecing, cut 3 strips 3½″ × width of fabric; subcut into 24 squares 3½″ × 3½″. Cut the squares in half diagonally.

- Cut 2 strips 2½″ × width of fabric; subcut into 8 rectangles 2½″ × 5½″. Set aside for paper piecing.

Background

- Cut 1 strip 8¾″ × width of fabric; subcut into 4 squares 8¾″ × 8¾″. Cut the squares in half diagonally.

- Cut 1 strip 6½″ × width of fabric; subcut into 4 squares 6½″ × 6½″. Cut the squares in half diagonally.

- Cut 2 strips 7⅝″ × width of fabric; subcut into 2 rectangles 7⅝″ × 28½″.

- Cut 1 strip 11½″ × 38″ for top border.

- Cut 1 strip 4½″ × 33½″ for right-hand border.

- Cut 3 strips 3½″ × width of fabric; subcut into 24 squares 3½″ × 3½″. Cut the squares in half diagonally and reserve for paper piecing.

Feathered Star Block Assembly

Center Lone Star

1 Piece the strip sets together, offsetting each strip by about 1¼″. **Fig. A**

2 Using the 45° marking on your ruler, trim the edge of the strip sets. **Fig. B**

3 Cut 8 strips 1¾″ wide from each strip set. **Fig. C**

4 Sew the strips together following the diamond unit assembly diagram to make 8 diamond center units, paying careful attention to the fabric placement. To sew diamond strips together accurately, align them right sides together with the corners overhanging about ¼″. **Fig. D**

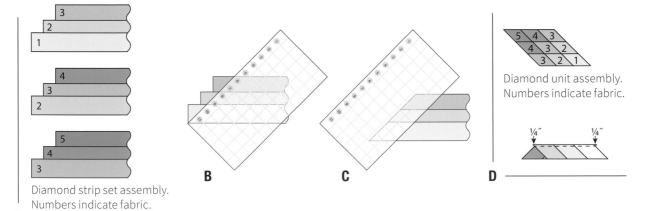

A Diamond strip set assembly. Numbers indicate fabric.

B

C

D Diamond unit assembly. Numbers indicate fabric.

Feathered Sections

1 Make 8 copies of patterns A and B (page 33) and paper piece, using fabric 6 and the background fabric where indicated. See Paper Piecing (page 103). Trim and remove papers.

2 Add the paper-pieced segments to the edges of each diamond unit, beginning with segment B and completing the diamond units with segment A. **Fig. E**

3 Following the block assembly diagram, add the 8¾″ and 6½″ triangles, paying careful attention to the size and orientation of the triangles. Make 4. **Fig. F**

4 Sew the block together by joining the 4 sections, as shown in the block assembly diagram. **Fig. G**

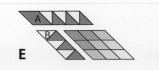

E

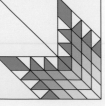

F

G Block assembly

Quilt Assembly

1. This block will be rotated 15°. Cut the 2 rectangles 7⅝″ × 28½″ in half diagonally to make 4 setting triangles. **Fig. H**

2. Sew the setting triangles onto the block, aligning the wider end with the corner of the block. The sharp corner of the setting triangle will overhang the edge of the block significantly. Trim this corner flush with the block after sewing. **Fig. I**

3. Add the 4½″ × 33½″ strip to the right side of the block. Sew the 11½″ × 38″ strip to the top of the block. Then trim the top down to 33½″ × 39½″ (or whatever size you prefer), beginning your measurements in the top right-hand corner and cutting off the left and bottom points of the feathered star in the process. **Fig. J**

TIP

You can also trim after quilting, if you prefer. You'll have to do a little extra quilting on the left and bottom of the quilt, but trimming after quilting makes for a fabulously square quilt.

H

Dashed line indicates cutting line.

1¼″

I

J

Quilt assembly

Finishing

1 Layer and quilt as desired.

2 To finish your quilt, cut 4 strips of facing fabric 2½″ × width of fabric.

3 Cut 2 strips 33½″ (or the actual width of your quilt after quilting), and 2 strips 38½″ long (or about 1″ shorter than the actual length of your quilt after quilting). Press in half lengthwise as for a typical binding.

4 With raw edges aligned, place the 33½″ strips onto the top and bottom edges of the front of the quilt and pin.

5 With raw edges aligned, center the 38½″ strips along the length of the front sides of the quilt and pin. These strips should overlap the strips placed in Step 4, as shown in the diagram (at right), but should not extend all the way to the corners of the quilt.

6 Stitch around the perimeter of the quilt top ¼″ from the edge, stopping to pivot at corners, as indicated by the dashed line. **Fig. K**

7 Clip the corners of the quilt, clipping backing and batting very close to facing stitching line.

8 Turn the facing toward the back, pressing with a hot iron as needed, and hand stitch to back.

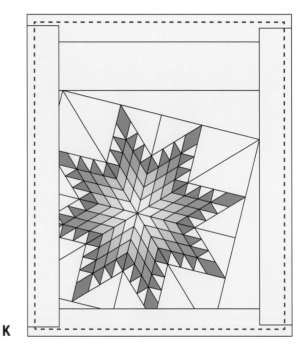

K

I quilted my quilt with straight lines and feathers that echo the star shape in the negative space and with curves and swirls inside the pieced block.

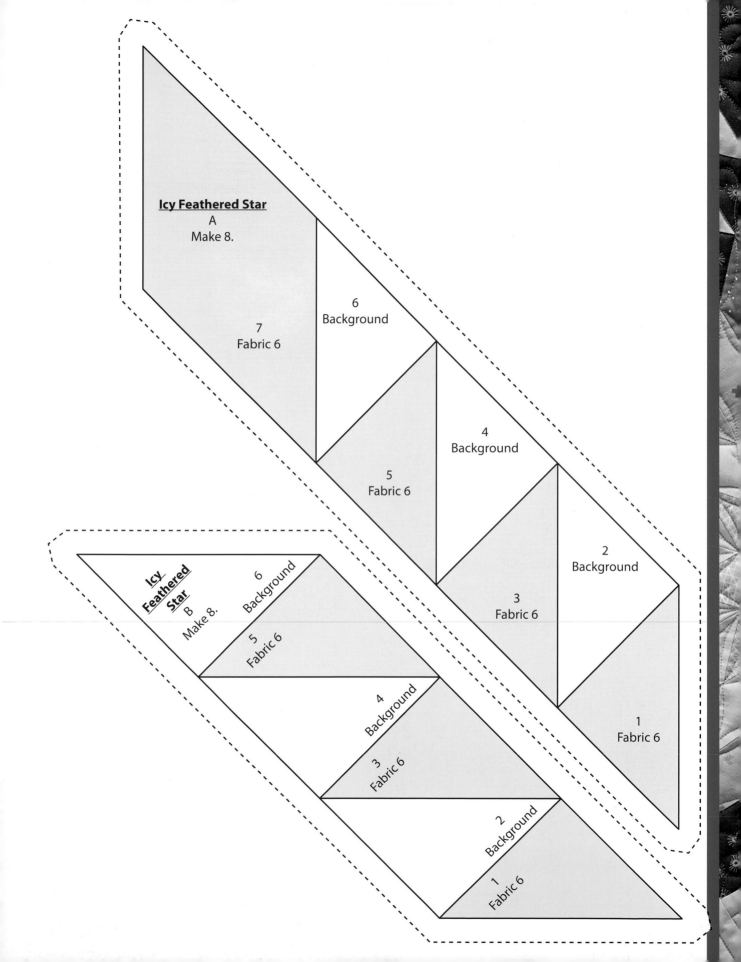

Icy Feathered Star
A
Make 8.

7
Fabric 6

6
Background

5
Fabric 6

4
Background

3
Fabric 6

2
Background

1
Fabric 6

Icy Feathered Star
B
Make 8.

6
Background

5
Fabric 6

4
Background

3
Fabric 6

2
Background

1
Fabric 6

4

Oversized Simple Blocks and Inverting

Chapter 3 discussed allowing complex blocks to stand on their own in a quilt design, but what if your favorite block is a small and simple one?

Oversized Blocks

If your block already has at least some background space built in—such as a Churn Dash—you could simply enlarge it!

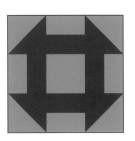

If you need a very quick quilt, or you are looking to explore minimalism in your quilting, you could blow this block up to a giant size and make

a quilt with one oversized simple block. This instantly creates negative space in what was just the block background. Small borders were added here to provide a little space between the block and the binding, but you could just make one giant block and be done with it.

Chapter 3 discussed placing your block partially off the edge of the quilt, and this is certainly a possibility with oversized simple blocks as well for a truly minimalist feel.

If this is too minimalist for you, you might want to play with repeating the block in a smaller scale across the whole quilt and creating the larger design with your fabric choices.

That has become a little busy, so you could change the original oversize block section back to a solid for a composition that gives the eye a place to rest.

Inverting Blocks

What is the foreground and what is the negative space in the previous design? The viewer's attention shifts from one area of the quilt to another, and inverting your blocks is a good way to play with this question. Traditional quilt blocks are often thought of as being made with darker fabrics on a light background, but what if you do something unexpected and reverse this?

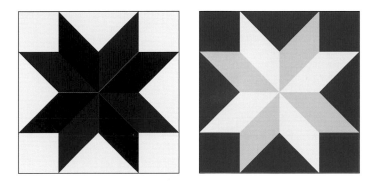

These two blocks create a very different effect, and inverting the block is quite striking. Again, you can make this block bigger, and you may wish to piece the background with the same or a related quilt block. This design keeps the slight color variation in the center quilt block, but you could also piece the center star in a single color.

The quilt blocks so far have all been simple, but inverting also works for more complicated quilt blocks, often in surprising ways. Take a look at a traditional Mariner's Compass block.

To invert this quilt block, you could begin by simply swapping white and blue areas, ignoring the variation in shades of blue.

You have created a ring of curvy triangles, which feels like an entirely new block full of possibilities!

There is also an interesting sun shape in the middle; you can emphasize this by making the outer curved setting pieces of the block the same color as the triangles.

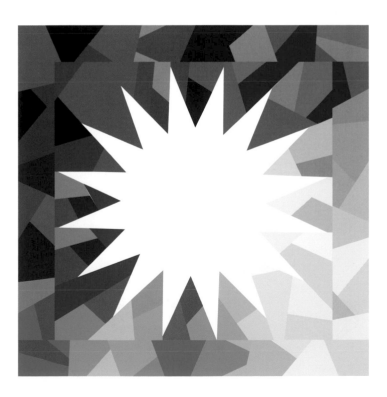

Just for fun, you could add some piecing to the background, too, but how about trying some improvisational piecing instead of repeating the quilt block on a smaller scale?

In this example, I have added some borders, too.

What is the negative space in this design? There is an argument to be made both for the solid white sun and for the scrappy rainbow surrounding it. You might find yourself pondering it if you make the quilt *Rainbow Sun* (page 38).

Rainbow Sun

Invert a Mariner's Compass block and improv piece the background for a striking mini quilt, using up all your smallest scraps in the process!

Finished block:
15″ × 15″

Finished quilt:
19½″ × 19½″

Made by Sylvia Schaefer, 2017

I echoed the sun shape using hand quilting with matching perle cotton #8 thread.

Materials

White solid: ⅜ yard for center sun

Rainbow scraps: About ¾ yard total

Lightweight interfacing or water-soluble stabilizer: 4½″ × 4½″ scrap

Batting: 27″ × 27″

Backing: ¾ yard

Binding: ¼ yard

Cutting

White solid

- Cut 1 strip 8″ × width of fabric; subcut into 16 rectangles 8″ × 2½″.

- Cut 1 circle pattern (page 40).

Interfacing or stabilizer

- Cut 1 circle pattern (page 40).

Piecing

Improv Piecing

Refer to the instructions for Improvisational Piecing (page 109) to make improv-pieced sections of fabric in the following sizes and colors. These will be used with the paper-piecing patterns in the next step.

Section 2: Make 4 sections 4″ × 3½″, 1 each in the following colors: dark blue, burgundy, yellow-orange, and dark green.

Section 4: Make 4 sections 4½″ × 4½″, 1 each in the following colors: light blue, reddish purple, orange, and green.

Section 6: Make 4 sections 5½″ × 5½″, 1 each in the following colors: dark aqua, purple, red-orange, and yellow-green.

Section 8: Make 4 sections 4½″ × 4½″, 1 each in the following colors: light aqua, violet, red, and yellow.

Paper Piecing

1 Make 4 copies of paper-piecing pattern B (page 41). Assign each copy a letter, A through D. Highlight or circle the corresponding colors on each copy to help you stay organized!

2 Following the instructions on Piecing Segments (page 105), paper piece each section, alternating between the precut white solid rectangles and the improvisationally pieced fabrics, as indicated.

3 Join the 4 sections together. There will be a hole in the center at this point. Remove the papers. **Fig. A**

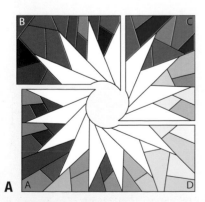

Add the Center Circle

1 Place the center white solid circle on top of the interfacing or stabilizer, right side down. Sew a ¼˝ seam all the way around the edge, backstitching at the beginning and end to secure. **Fig. B**

2 Carefully cut a slit in the interfacing layer only, then turn the circle inside out and press.

3 Appliqué the circle to the center of the paper-pieced section using a zigzag or invisible machine appliqué stitch and matching thread. **Fig. C**

Add the Borders

1 Following the instructions on Improvisational Piecing (page 109), piece a strip at least 19½˝ × 2½˝ using fabrics that shift from purple to red-orange. Trim to 19½˝ × 2½˝. **Fig. D**

2 Piece a strip at least 19½˝ × 2½˝ using fabrics that shift from dark aqua to yellow-green. Trim to 19½˝ × 2½˝. **Fig. E**

3 Piece a strip at least 15½˝ × 2½˝ using fabrics that shift from red-orange to yellow-green. Trim to 15½˝ × 2½˝. **Fig. F**

4 Piece a strip at least 15½˝ × 2½˝ using fabrics that shift from purple to dark aqua. Trim to 15½˝ × 2½˝. **Fig. G**

5 Attach the borders to the quilt top following the quilt assembly diagram. **Fig. H**

Finishing

Layer, quilt, and bind as desired.

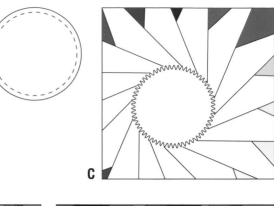

Quilt assembly

Rainbow Sun
Cut 1 from white.

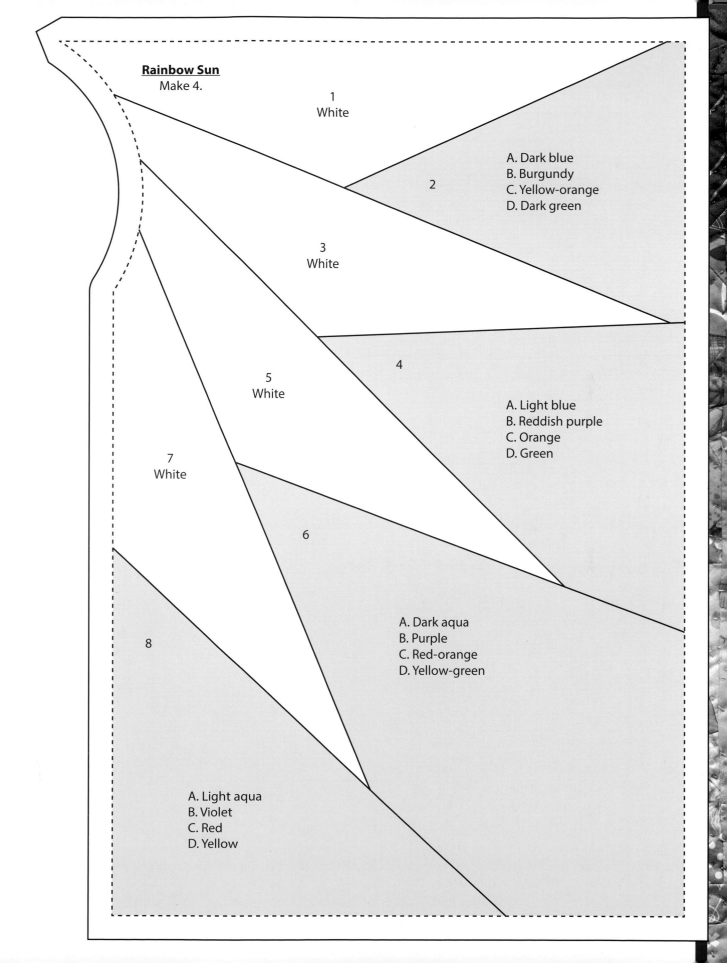

Rainbow Sun
Make 4.

1
White

2

A. Dark blue
B. Burgundy
C. Yellow-orange
D. Dark green

3
White

4

5
White

A. Light blue
B. Reddish purple
C. Orange
D. Green

7
White

6

A. Dark aqua
B. Purple
C. Red-orange
D. Yellow-green

8

A. Light aqua
B. Violet
C. Red
D. Yellow

5 Setting Rows

Aside from setting a single block on its own in a quilt, one of the simplest ways to incorporate negative space into a quilt design is to set only a few rows of blocks in a quilt top and leave the rest as background. This is an excellent choice for highlighting relatively simple blocks. It also works particularly well for blocks that create interesting secondary patterns when set in a traditional grid layout.

The Rule of Thirds

While it can be interesting to have a line of blocks run along the center of your quilt, keep in mind the Rule of Thirds. If you have dabbled in photography at all—or even just read one of those "10 Ways To Take Better iPhone Photos" articles on the internet—you have probably heard of this rule. Essentially, it states that the major lines in a photograph or design should fall onto horizontal and vertical lines dividing the space into thirds. Consider the following two photos. Which is more interesting?

Photos by Sylvia Schaefer

In the second photo (above right), the important lines (the tree, the shoreline) fall onto or near the lines dividing the photo into thirds.

The same rule can be applied to quilt design. Asymmetry is often far more interesting than symmetry, and it tends to create more of a sense of motion and dynamism. Which of the following two designs—identical except for a small difference in the placement of the band of blocks—do you prefer?

Notice how the asymmetrical placement of the rows on the above left quilt lends weight to the bottom of the quilt. In general, placing the center line of your rows on one of the "thirds lines" works well. This quilt is based on the traditional Left and Right block (see the pattern in *Row of Diamonds*, page 46).

Setting and Adjusting Rows

Typically, unless your block is particularly complex, several rows of blocks create the best design. This is particularly true if you are using blocks that create secondary designs, as you will often not see the secondary design when setting only one row of blocks. The Jupiter block is a good example.

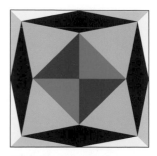

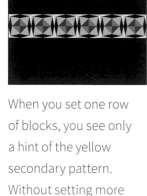
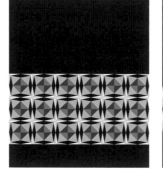
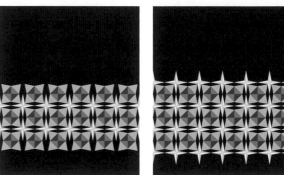

When you set one row of blocks, you see only a hint of the yellow secondary pattern. Without setting more rows the full pattern isn't evident.

With three rows, on the other hand, the secondary pattern takes center stage.

In many cases, you will need to recolor or add elements to the outer rows of your quilt design so that the edge of the rows is not so abrupt and the blocks and the background interlock. Here, you have two options: removing the top and bottom yellow star halves or adding in the missing halves to the rows above and below the band of blocks.

The far right design works better in this case because it emphasizes the narrow yellow stars and finishes off the rows nicely.

How Many Blocks?

The number of blocks to set will primarily be a factor of the size of the blocks and the desired size of your quilt. In general, if the block is simple, you will probably want more than if the block is complex. Another general rule of design is that odd numbers tend to be more interesting than even numbers, so consider the focus of your design. The example above contains six blocks across the quilt, but because the secondary pattern is the focus of the design and setting six blocks creates five full iterations of the secondary pattern, an even number of blocks worked. This chapter's pattern quilt (*Row of Diamonds*, page 46; also see the block on page 43), on the other hand, uses five blocks in each horizontal row.

More Ways to Set Rows

The lines you set your blocks in can be vertical, horizontal, diagonal, or even at an odd angle. Consider how the following quilt design changes as you change the direction of the line of blocks. Which one do you prefer?

The blocks in the horizontal and vertical designs have been set on point. Sometimes, the spacing looks better this way, particularly for circular block designs, so keep this in mind as an option.

Finally, you can also leave empty spaces within your lines of blocks, particularly if your blocks are small. In *Paper Cranes*, a quilt inspired by Japanese origami, I offset the columns of blocks and left some spaces empty to add negative space within the lines of blocks, too.

Paper Cranes, by Sylvia Schaefer, 40˝ × 52˝, 2014

Row of Diamonds

A simple row of blocks is a great way to feature favorite prints—choose a line of fabrics by one designer, or mix them up from your stash as I did here!

Finished block:
5″ × 5″

Finished quilt:
46½″ × 55½″

Made by Sylvia Schaefer, 2016

Materials

Berry solid: 1⅝ yards for background

White solid: ¾ yard for accent

Assorted prints: 1⅛ yards total for feature fabrics

Batting: 54″ × 63″

Backing: 3 yards

Binding: ½ yard

5″ square ruler (*optional*)

Cutting

Berry solid

- Cut 1 strip parallel to selvage 28″ × 45½″ for the top border.

- Cut 1 strip parallel to selvage 9½″ × 45½″ for the bottom border.

- Cut 1 strip 6″ × width of fabric; subcut into 10 rectangles 4″ × 6″.

White solid

- Cut 12 strips 1¾″ × width of fabric; subcut into 60 strips 1¾″ × 7″.

Assorted prints

- Cut 50 rectangles 4″ × 6″.

Block Assembly

1 Sort the 4″ × 6″ rectangles into 2 equal piles, each containing 5 background rectangles and 25 feature rectangles. Cut the rectangles in half diagonally, being careful to cut the 2 piles in opposite directions. **Fig. A**

2 Working with 1 pile at a time, sew 1 white accent strip and 1 newly created triangle right sides together, lining them up so that the sharpest corner of the triangle overhangs by ¾″. **Fig. B**

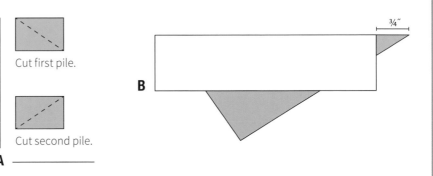

Cut first pile.

Cut second pile.

A

¾″

B

3 Press the seams toward the dark. Align another rectangle from the same pile with the other side of the white accent strip. Again, allow the sharpest corner to hang off the opposite edge by ¾″, and stitch. **Fig. C**

TIP

Press the seams away from the white accent strip to avoid unsightly shadow-through of the darker fabrics. If you have chosen a different color scheme and shadow-through is not a concern, you can press the seams toward the accent strip on one set of blocks and away from the accent strip on the other to allow your seams to nest when sewing blocks together.

4 Press, and trim the block to 5″ square by lining up the markings ¼″ inside opposite corners of your ruler with the outside seams (where the strips meet the triangles), as shown in the diagram. If you don't have a 5″ square ruler, place some painter's or washi tape on your larger ruler marking the lines at 4¾″ to help you line up the seams. Trim 2 sides at a time, then rotate the block and trim the other 2 sides. **Fig. D**

5 Make 30 blocks, 10 of which will have 1 triangle of background fabric paired with 1 triangle of feature fabric. Repeat with the second pile of fabrics that were cut in the opposite direction. **Fig. E**

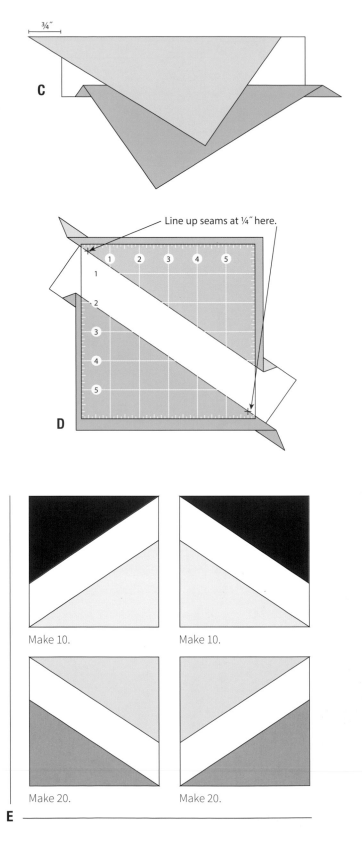

Make 10.

Make 10.

Make 20.

Make 20.

Quilt Assembly

1. Following the block assembly diagram, assemble the blocks in 6 rows of 10, alternating the direction of the white strip to form diamonds and placing the blocks that include background fabric in the top and bottom rows. **Fig. F**

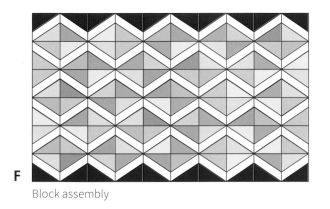

F

Block assembly

2. Sew the wide (28˝) strip of background to the top of the row of blocks. Sew the narrower (9½˝) strip to the bottom of the row of blocks. **Fig. G**

G

Quilt assembly

Finishing

Layer, quilt, and bind as desired.

By using a walking foot to carry the zigzag lines across the whole quilt, the quilting ties together the negative space and the blocks. I then quilted a variety of free-motion designs in the diamond shapes.

6 Scattering

Another approach to setting smaller quilt blocks is to distribute them across the quilt top, leaving negative space in between. This seems to work particularly well with blocks that are representational (that is, they depict an object, such as an animal or a tree) because it mimics the way you often find objects in the natural world.

What Is and Isn't Random

To better understand the way in which you can distribute blocks across a quilt top, take a moment to think about randomness. Shown below are three different quilt designs; each is made up of 25 butterfly blocks. In which one would you say that the butterflies are placed randomly?

Most people will choose the middle image. The left is obviously organized in rows and columns. The right has that big cluster of butterflies and that can't happen just by chance—or can it?

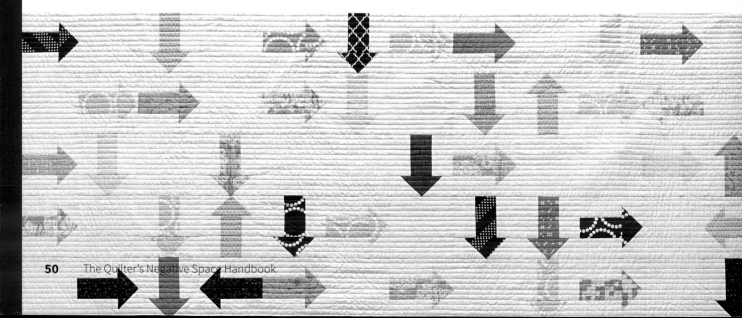

Here are the three designs again, but this time with a 5 × 5 grid overlaid, which corresponds to a set of 25 Nine-Patch blocks.

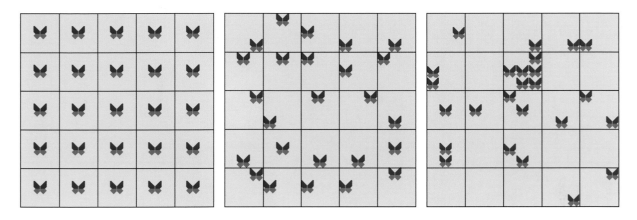

You can now see that indeed, in the far left quilt, the butterfly is in the center of each Nine-Patch. In the middle quilt, there is only one butterfly per Nine-Patch block, but it has been randomly placed within that block. This is what statisticians call a "distributed random" layout, because it is only partially random—you are still forcing a relatively even distribution of butterflies. The far right quilt is the truly random layout; I created it simply by generating 25 unique random numbers between 1 and 225 (the total number of possible locations) and placing the butterfly blocks accordingly. When the grid is overlaid, you can see that sometimes you end up with no butterflies in a Nine-Patch unit; sometimes you end up with many.

We humans are inclined to try to find patterns whenever we can, even when none exist. A relatively even scattering of items appears much more haphazard than when we can see groupings. As a quilter, you can use this knowledge to your advantage. When trying to create a random look, you will often want to use what is really a distributed random layout. Quilters tend to do this naturally when arranging blocks on their design wall. However, if your block is something like a butterfly, try starting with an online random number generator for your layout, as animals do cluster and this might create a more natural look for your quilt. (Obviously, animal clusters tend not to be a result of random chance, but that's a tale for another time!)

Adding Additional Interest

You might have looked at the butterfly quilt designs (page 51) and thought that they need something else. There are a couple different ways to add additional interest to a quilt with blocks scattered across it.

Adding Ghost Blocks

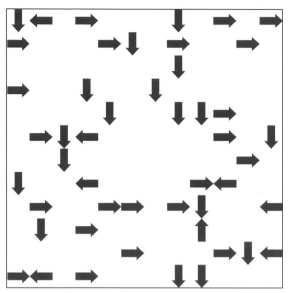

Here is an example of a quilt using arrow blocks; the initial positions of the blocks were determined using a random number generator (a true random layout). I then rotated some as I saw fit.

The first thing you might want to do with this design is add another color. Perhaps change some of the blocks to aqua, complementing the bright purple?

This already adds a great deal of interest, but the layout still appears a bit haphazard. Adding more bright purple or aqua blocks could overwhelm the design, but what if you fill in the empty spaces with more muted arrows, such as grays? These sorts of "ghost" or "shadow" blocks can help unify a design without making it too busy.

Find the pattern for this quilt at the end of the chapter (*Every Which Way*, page 54).

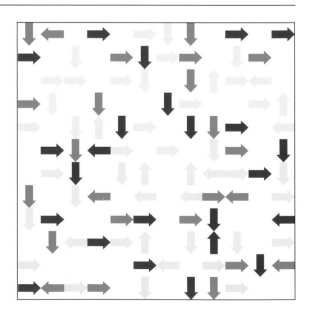

Adding a Focal Point

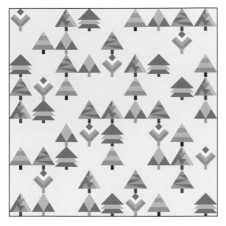

Another option in a scattered quilt layout is the addition of a focal point. Consider this little forest. The design is based on a distributed random layout.

While this layout works okay on its own, a focal point will help hold your viewer's attention for longer.

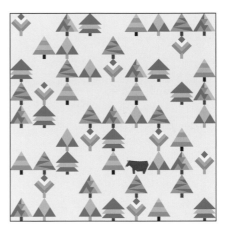

Such a focal point doesn't necessarily have to be large. For example, adding a little bear roaming the woods might be just the touch of added charm you need. It's a good idea, when placing these sorts of focal points, to keep The Rule of Thirds (page 42) in mind.

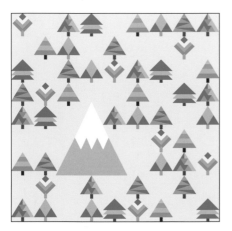

However, a larger focal point works well too. Maybe your forest surrounds a mountain? You could also try a lake if you are willing to tackle a curved element.

NOTE | *Remember the discussion from Chapter 2 about varying block sizes (page 17), too.*

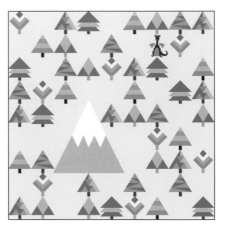

You can also include both a small and a large focal point. This helps to lead the viewer's eye across the quilt and creates a charming little story for the quilt. Perhaps, instead of a bear, a magical creature lives beneath your mountain and roams its forests?

Every Which Way

Scatter soft gray arrows amongst the brightly colored ones to make your placement look deliberate. This quilt is scrap-friendly—use a soft uniform print for the negative space as done here, or try a scrappy low-volume look!

Finished block:
6″ × 6″

Finished quilt:
72½″ × 72½″

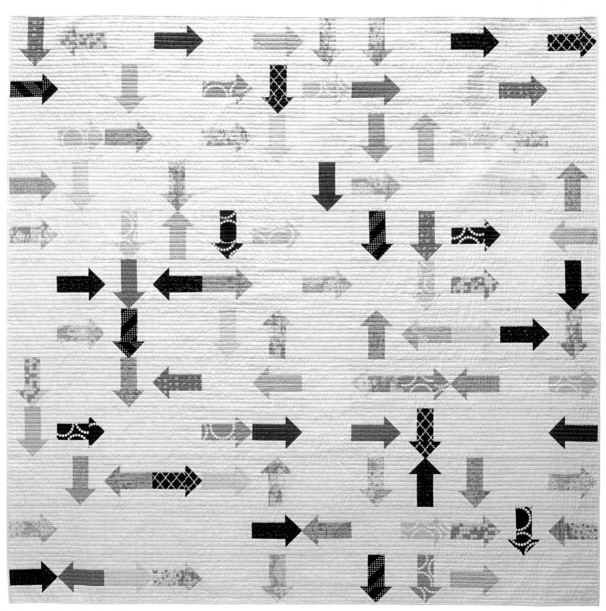

Made by Sylvia Schaefer, 2017

Materials

Low-volume print:
4⅜ yards for background

Assorted teals:
6 fat eighths for arrow blocks

Assorted purples:
6 fat eighths for arrow blocks

Assorted grays:
¼ yard each of 6 fabrics for arrow blocks

Batting: 80″ × 80″

Backing: 4½ yards

Binding: ⅝ yard

Cutting

Background (low-volume print)

- Cut 8 strips 2⅞″ × width of fabric; subcut into 96 squares 2⅞″ × 2⅞″.

- Cut 8 strips 6½″ × width of fabric; subcut into 48 squares 6½″ × 6½″.

- Cut 12 strips 4½″ × width of fabric; subcut into 192 rectangles 2½″ × 4½″.

- Cut 12 strips 1½″ × width of fabric; subcut into 192 rectangles 2½″ × 1½″.

Assorted teals (6)

- From each fabric, cut 1 square 5¼″ × 5¼″ and 4 rectangles 2½″ × 4½″, for a total of 6 squares and 24 rectangles.

Assorted purples (6)

- From each fabric, cut 1 square 5¼″ × 5¼″ and 4 rectangles 2½″ × 4½″, for a total of 6 squares and 24 rectangles.

Assorted grays (6)

- From each fabric, cut 2 squares 5¼″ × 5¼″ and 8 rectangles 2½″ × 4½″, for a total of 12 squares and 48 rectangles.

Block Assembly

Flying Geese Units

1 To make sets of 4 Flying Geese at a time, take 1 colored 5¼″ square and 4 background 2⅞″ squares. Using a pencil or erasable fabric pen and a ruler, draw diagonal lines across all the background squares. Place 2 squares as shown and sew ¼″ from the line (dashed lines) on both sides. **Fig. A**

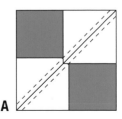

2 Cut along the marked line and press toward the dark. **Fig. B**

3 Place another 2⅞″ background square on top of each unit as shown, and sew ¼″ from the marked line on both sides (indicated by the dashed line). **Fig. C**

4 Cut along the marked line and press toward the dark. Trim the corners. Each unit should measure 4½″ × 2½″. Repeat for a total of 24 each of teal and purple Flying Geese units and 48 gray Flying Geese units. **Fig. D**

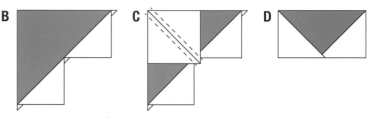

Arrow Assembly

1 Sew a 2½″ × 4½″ background rectangle to both sides of each colored 2½″ × 4½″ rectangle , pressing as indicated by the arrows.

2 Sew a 1½″ × 2½″ background rectangle to both sides of each Flying Geese unit.

3 Sew the 2 halves of the block together, ensuring that the prints match. **Fig. E**

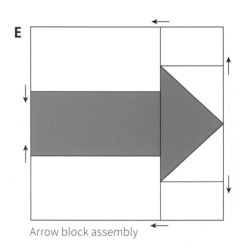

Arrow block assembly

Quilt Assembly

Join the rows of the quilt following the assembly diagram, interspersing plain 6½″ squares. Sew columns together, paying attention to the direction of the blocks. **Fig. F**

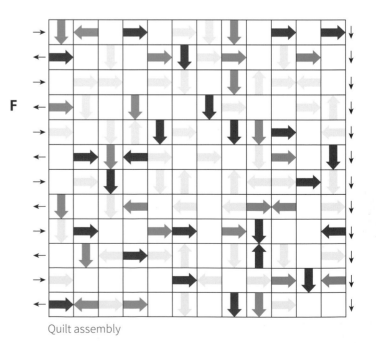

Quilt assembly

Finishing

Layer, quilt, and bind as desired.

The straight-line quilting emphasizes the directionality implied by the arrows.

7 Disintegration

Creating a sense of deconstruction or disintegration across your quilt can create a great deal of motion in your design, as it implies that some force is causing your blocks to come apart. You can approach creating such a design in two ways—by using parts of a single block or by using multiples of the same block across your whole quilt.

Disintegration in a Single Block

If you want to use only one block in your disintegrating design, it is best to choose a relatively complex block, particularly one that has repeated elements.

This is an example of a complex block. Notice the repeated triangles in the design.

You could start by surrounding the block with negative space as discussed in Chapter 3 (page 26). The block is, again, placed roughly in accordance with The Rule of Thirds (page 42). However, this design could benefit from something more.

There are a lot of repeated triangles in this block, and by moving some of them out of their positions and allowing the rosette to disintegrate, you can create a sense of motion in the quilt. This is an improvement, but it might leave you wondering what's happening in all that negative space to cause the block to disintegrate.

By adding a second, smaller version of the block, you create a sense of connection and a story for the quilt.

This sort of piecing can be a little challenging. Improvisational piecing is a good way to approach it, but be aware that improvisational piecing gets harder the larger your quilt top because of the need to keep cuts straight and to accurately judge the size of pieces to be inserted. Matching parts of the quilt that are sewn in different sections can also be challenging, and you may end up needing to join awkwardly shaped sections by hand or with Y-seams. Purchase plenty of extra background fabric when planning this type of quilt. You may also wish to consider whether appliquéing your shapes might be an easier and/or more efficient method of achieving this look.

Disintegration Using Multiple Blocks

The other option for creating disintegration in your quilt design is to repeat a single block (or portions of a block). The key is to create a gradient across your quilt top. As a result, this approach is best for simpler, smaller blocks that can easily be pieced on a relatively small scale since you need a fairly large number of blocks to make this effect adequately apparent.

At its most basic, you can create a gradient with careful fabric placement. *Corona* uses only half-square triangle blocks, with fabrics placed into a gradient.

Corona, by Sylvia Schaefer, 40″ × 52″, 2017

Now consider a slightly more complex block, a Churn Dash.

You could arrange this block in a gradient across your quilt, such that one side has more blocks than the other. In this case, most of the blocks are at the bottom, with fewer blocks toward the top.

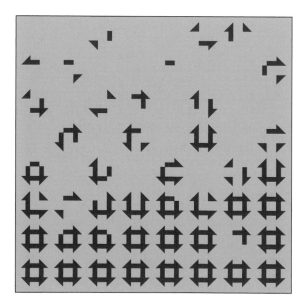

This creates an interesting effect of blocks floating away from a pool of them at the bottom of the quilt. You can further emphasize this by eliminating some of the rectangles and triangles making up each Churn Dash block. Here, a few more partial Churn Dash blocks were added to the top of the quilt so as not to leave the top portion of the quilt looking too sparse.

What you might call "multi-part" blocks, or blocks with a number of separate elements, are also great for this type of design. This traditional block called Red Peony Buds has diamonds and on-point squares that could be separated out.

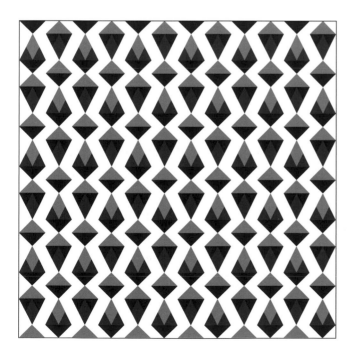

As you can probably see, this block is intended to be tiled to create a continuous pattern. However, doing so creates an overly busy quilt without any real focus.

It does, however, create an interesting secondary pattern—the white zigzag between the shapes—that would be a shame to lose entirely, so scattering the block pieces across the quilt, as discussed in Chapter 6 (page 50), wouldn't be as effective in this design. Instead, you can try removing shapes in a gradient pattern to create something like this.

This design might remind you of the sort of video game where you have to clear jewels from a game board! A little recoloring and you have the quilt pattern for the project *Jewel Drop* (next page).

In the last two examples of disintegration using multiples of a block, one design (the Churn Dash, page 60) takes the gradient across the quilt, from bottom to top, and the other goes diagonally across the quilt. You might want to try a gradient from side to side or from the center outward.

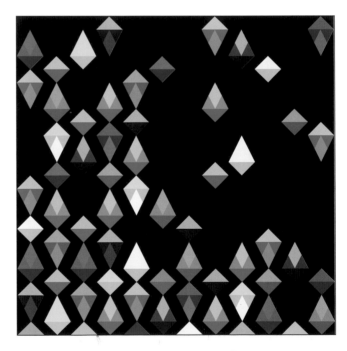

With the quilt using Churn Dash blocks, you started out by placing a gradient of blocks across the quilt. In the Red Peony Buds example (beginning on page 61), you started by placing blocks across the entire quilt, and then removed elements of those blocks. Either approach is a valid way of achieving the same result.

Jewel Drop

*By breaking up the inspiration block and placing elements in a
gradient, this quilt is reminiscent of a jewel-clearing arcade game.
Choose six coordinating colors with light, medium, and dark hues
of each for the candy-colored jewels.*

Finished block:
6″ × 6″

Finished quilt:
72½″ × 72½″

Made by Sylvia Schaefer, 2017

Materials

Black solid: 4 yards for background

Light fabrics (6 colors): ¼ yard each for blocks

Medium fabrics (6 colors): ⅛ yard each for blocks

Dark fabrics (6 colors): ¼ yard each for blocks

Batting: 80″ × 80″

Backing: 4½ yards

Binding: ⅝ yard

Template plastic: 1 sheet

White chalk marking pen

Cutting

• *Make templates:* Trace patterns A, B, and C (page 67) onto template plastic and cut out.

Black solid

• Cut 10 strips 4″ × width of fabric; subcut into 96 squares 4″ × 4″.

• Cut 9 strips 3½″ × width of fabric. Cut 42 pieces, using template C; then flip the template over and cut 42 reverse pieces.

• Cut 10 strips 6½″ × width of fabric; subcut according to chart. For best fabric usage, see the cutting diagram (below).

LETTER	CUT SIZE	NUMBER NEEDED
A	3½″ × 6½″	3
B	6½″ × 6½″	3
C	9½″ × 6½″	8
D	12½″ × 6½″	1
E	15½″ × 6½″	4
F	18½″ × 6½″	1
G	21½″ × 6½″	1
H	24½″ × 6½″	3
I	33½″ × 6½″	1
J	45½″ × 6½″	1*

* Use leftovers from another strip to piece.

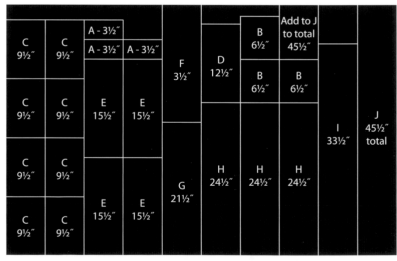

Cutting diagram for background fabric. All strips are 6½″ wide.

Light fabrics (6)

• Cut 2 squares 7½″ × 7½″ from each.

• From the remainder, cut 4 pieces from each, using template A.

Medium fabrics (6)

• Cut 3 pieces from each, using template A.

• Cut 8 pieces from each, using template B.

Dark fabrics (6)

• Cut 2 squares 7½″ × 7½″ from each.

• From the remainder, cut 6 pieces from each, using template B.

Block Assembly

Flying Geese Units

1 To make sets of 4 Flying Geese at a time, take 1 colored 7½″ square and 4 black 4″ squares. Using the chalk marking pen and a ruler, draw diagonal lines across all the black background squares. Place as shown and sew ¼″ from the line (on the dashed lines) on both sides. **Fig. A**

2 Cut along the marked line and press toward the dark. **Fig. B**

3 Place another 4″ black background square on top of each unit, and sew ¼″ from the marked line on both sides. **Fig. C**

4 Cut along the marked line and press toward the dark. Trim to 6½″ × 3½″. **Fig. D**

5 Repeat for all 7¼″ squares, for a total of 8 Flying Geese units from each color (96 total).

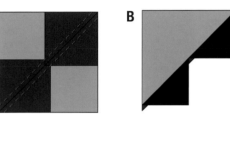

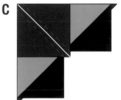

Jewel Blocks

Jewel blocks are assembled from pieces cut using the templates. You will make 2 variants of blocks from each color: a light/medium and a medium/dark.

1 Join a B triangle to adjacent sides of the A diamond, then sew C triangles to the unit. Make 4 each of light/medium units for each color and 3 each of medium/dark units for each color. **Fig. E**

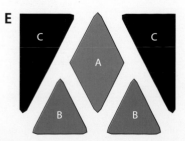

2   Join the dark Flying Geese
    to each of the light/medium
    block units. Press toward
    the Flying Geese. **Fig. F**

3   Join the light Flying Geese
    to each of the medium/dark
    units. Press toward the
    Flying Geese. **Fig. G**

On-Point Square Blocks

From each color family, take
3 light and 3 dark Flying Geese
units and join them together to
make on-point square blocks.
Press toward the dark. **Fig. H**

Quilt Assembly

Join the columns of the quilt
following the quilt assembly
diagram, then sew the columns
together. **Fig. I**

Finishing

Layer, quilt, and bind as
desired.

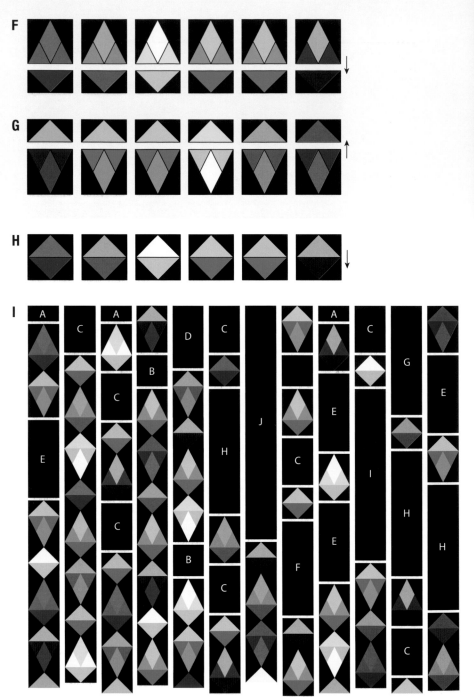

Quilt assembly

Echoing the jewel shapes in the negative space carries the design across the whole quilt and helps unify the negative and
positive space.

66   The Quilter's Negative Space Handbook

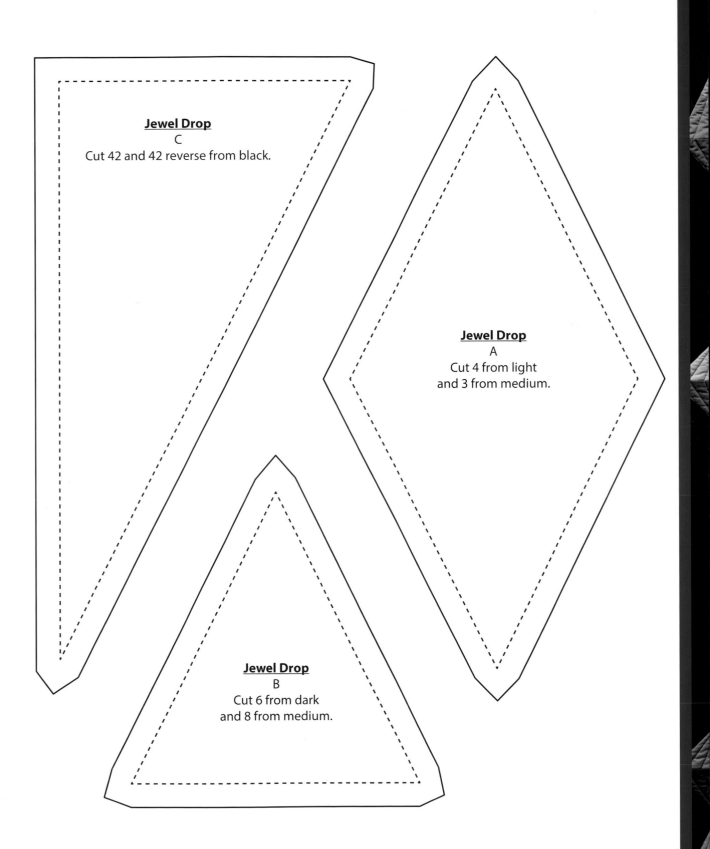

Jewel Drop
C
Cut 42 and 42 reverse from black.

Jewel Drop
A
Cut 4 from light
and 3 from medium.

Jewel Drop
B
Cut 6 from dark
and 8 from medium.

Making Shapes

In many ways, this is similar to the concept of inverting blocks (page 34) discussed in Chapter 4, since in that case you essentially created the shape of a block with your negative space. But let's set aside the idea of just enlarging a simple block and explore the idea of creating shapes with your negative space a little further.

Shapes Using Square Blocks

  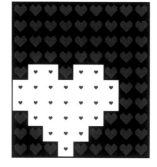 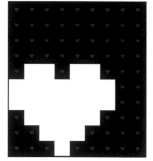

If you are a fan of the pixel quilt trend, you might have already played with this concept a little. Let's say you are inspired by a heart block.

For maximum cohesion in the quilt design, try choosing a shape inspired by the block. In this case, you could create a heart shape with your negative space and surround it with pieced heart blocks.

To create additional interest, you could consider adding tiny hearts in your large heart shape.

Alternatively, what if you kept the negative space white but shrunk down your outer hearts?

In this design, you are again playing with the question of what, exactly, is the negative space. An argument can be made for both the white heart and the dark red background—but either way, the dark red helps the white heart really pop.

Forming Curves

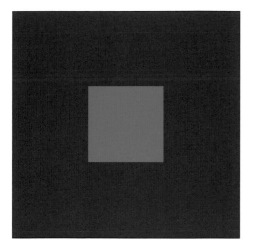

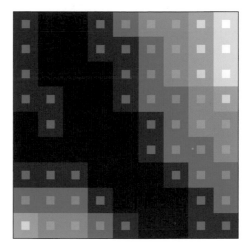

A heart is easy enough to approximate with square quilt blocks, but what if you want to make smoother curves? There are several approaches to this problem. Say you are inspired by a river and would like to create a stream running across your quilt, which will use a simple Square-in-a-Square block.

When you try to create a river shape with these blocks, it's a little too jagged to give you quite the right effect.

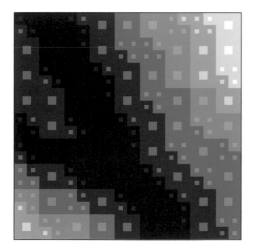

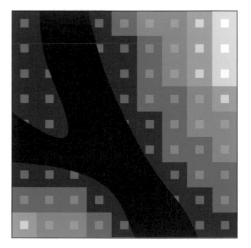

However, since this is a simple block, you could mix in blocks in a smaller size to help smooth the curve.

NOTE | *The pattern for this quilt—in a completely different colorway—is at the end of this chapter (**River of Fire,** page 72). Notice how the change in colors changes the focus of the design!*

If you truly want a smooth, organic look, you can certainly use appliqué or an improv curved piecing technique to make your negative space cut across the quilt without regard to the blocks.

You can also use patches within a block to smooth out the curve. Blocks that are designed to be repeated over an entire quilt and create secondary shapes are particularly good candidates for this type of treatment. These kinds of blocks, if they do not actually contain curves, often create the appearance of curves over a quilt top and can therefore be used to create more complex shapes. You have most likely seen this approach used with the Storm at Sea quilt block.

A block with curved elements provides even smoother shapes.

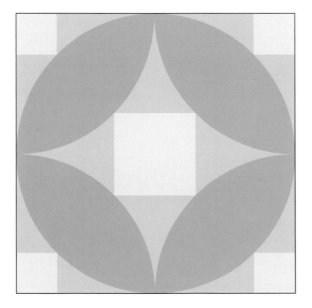

TIP

Add some appliquéd raindrops to complete the effect!

Alternative Block Shapes

Finally, don't forget to consider the possibilities of alternative block shapes when trying to create shapes with your negative space. Hexagons, diamonds, tumbler blocks … whether you make a one-patch quilt or piece your blocks, the possibilities for creating shapes are endless! Here are just a few of many possibilities using hexagon and diamond blocks.

River of Fire

This quilt creates the curving shape of a river by using blocks in two different sizes to smooth out the curves. Try this lava-inspired color scheme or the cool greens and blues shown in the chapter.

Finished block:
6″ × 6″

Finished quilt:
54½″ × 54½″

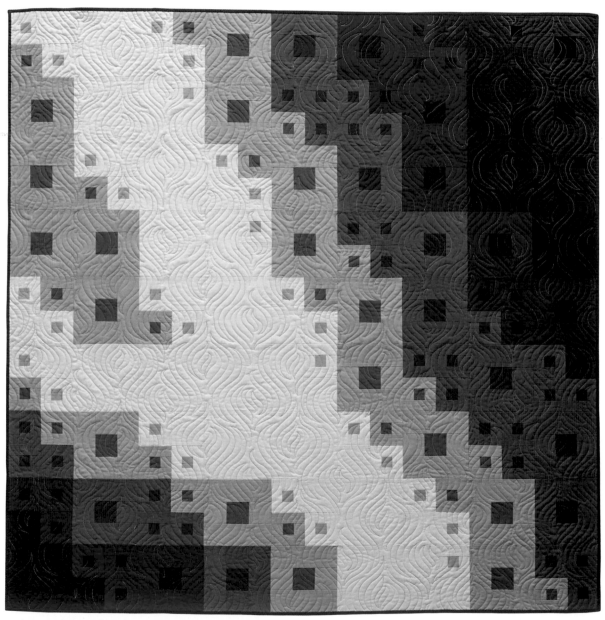

Made by Sylvia Schaefer, 2017

Materials

Bright yellow solid: 1¼ yards

Yellow-orange solid: 1⅛ yards

Red-orange solid: 1⅛ yards

Red solid: ¾ yard

Dark red solid: ⅜ yard

Dark gray solid: ⅜ yard

Black solid: ⅛ yard

Batting: 62˝ × 62˝

Backing: 3½ yards

Binding: ½ yard

Cutting

NOTE | *This quilt is constructed using a strip-piecing technique. Be sure to read the instructions before beginning, as you may be able to make fewer strip sets if your fabric is wider than 40˝. You may also wish to cut fabrics for a few blocks individually in order to avoid wasting fabric.*

Bright yellow solid

- Cut 2 strips 6½˝ × width of fabric; subcut into 12 squares 6½˝ × 6½˝.
- Cut 3 strips 3½˝ × width of fabric; subcut into 16 squares 3½˝ × 3½˝ and 4 strips 3½˝ × 6½˝.
- Cut 6 strips 1½˝ × width of fabric; subcut into 56 strips 1½˝ × 3½˝.
- Cut 4 strips 1½˝ × width of fabric for strip piecing. If you have 42˝ usable fabric for the width, cut 2.

Yellow-orange solid

- Cut 4 strips 1½˝ × width of fabric; subcut into 38 strips 1½˝ × 3½˝.
- Cut 6 strips 2½˝ × width of fabric; subcut into 34 strips 2½˝ × 6½˝.
- Cut 4 strips 1½˝ × width of fabric for strip piecing. If you have 40½˝ usable fabric for the width, cut 3.
- Cut 4 strips 2½˝ × width of fabric for strip piecing. If you have 42½˝ usable fabric for the width, cut 2.

Red-orange solid

- Cut 6 strips 1½˝ × width of fabric; subcut into 56 strips 1½˝ × 3½˝.
- Cut 3 strips 2½˝ × width of fabric; subcut into 18 strips 2½˝ × 6½˝.
- Cut 5 strips 1½˝ × width of fabric for strip piecing. If you have 42˝ usable fabric for the width, cut 3.
- Cut 4 strips 2½˝ × width of fabric for strip piecing. If you have 42½˝ usable fabric for the width, cut 3.

Red solid

- Cut 3 strips 1½˝ × width of fabric; subcut into 28 strips 1½˝ × 3½˝.
- Cut 2 strips 2½˝ × width of fabric; subcut into 12 strips 2½˝ × 6½˝.
- Cut 4 strips 1½˝ × width of fabric for strip piecing. If you have 42˝ usable fabric for the width, cut 3.
- Cut 3 strips 2½˝ × width of fabric for strip piecing.

Dark red solid

- Cut 2 strips 1½″ × width of fabric; subcut into 14 strips 1½″ × 3½″. Set the remainder aside for strip piecing.

- Cut 2 strips 2½″ × width of fabric; subcut into 8 strips 2½″ × 6½″. Set the remainder aside for strip piecing.

- Cut 1 strip 1½″ × width of fabric and 1 strip 2½″ × width of fabric for strip piecing.

Dark gray solid

- Cut 1 strip 1½″ × width of fabric; subcut into 8 strips 1½″ × 3½″. Set the remainder aside for strip piecing.

- Cut 1 strip 2½″ × width of fabric; subcut into 4 strips 2½″ × 6½″. Set the remainder aside for strip piecing.

- Cut 1 strips 1½″ × width of fabric and 1 strip 2½″ × width of fabric for strip piecing.

Black solid

- Cut 1 strip 1½″ × 7″ or longer and 1 strip 2½″ × 7″ or longer for strip piecing.

Strip Piecing

Bright Yellow and Yellow-Orange Strips

Piece a 1½″ × width of fabric strip of bright yellow to either side of a 1½″ × width of fabric strip of yellow-orange, pressing as indicated by the arrows. Make 2; make 1 if you have 42″ usable width. Subcut into 28 strips 1½″ × 3½″. **Fig. A**

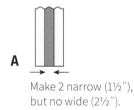

A

Make 2 narrow (1½″), but no wide (2½″).

Yellow-Orange and Red-Orange Strips

1 Piece a 1½″ × width of fabric strip of yellow-orange to either side of a 1½″ × width of fabric strip of red-orange. Subcut into 19 strips 1½″ × 3½″.

2 Piece a 2½″ × width of fabric strip of yellow-orange to either side of a 2½″ × width of fabric strip of red-orange. Make 2; make 1 if you have 42½″ usable width. Subcut into 17 strips 2½″ × 6½″. **Fig. B**

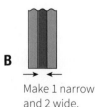

B

Make 1 narrow and 2 wide.

Red-Orange and Red Strips

1 Piece a 1½″ × width of fabric strip of red-orange to either side of a 1½″ × width of fabric strip of red. Make 2; make 1 if you have 42″ usable width. Subcut into 28 strips 1½″ × 3½″.

2 Piece a 2½″ × width of fabric strip of red-orange to either side of a 2½″ × width of fabric strip of red. Subcut into 9 strips 2½″ × 6½″. **Fig. C**

C

Make 2 narrow and 1 wide.

Red and Dark Red Strips

1 Piece a 1½″ × width of fabric strip of red to either side of a 1½″ × width of fabric strip of dark red. Subcut into 14 strips 1½″ × 3½″.

2 Piece a 2½″ × width of fabric strip of red to either side of a 2½″ × width of fabric strip of dark red. Subcut into 6 strips 2½″ × 6½″. **Fig. D**

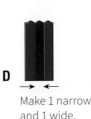

D

Make 1 narrow and 1 wide.

Dark Red and Dark Gray Strips

1 Cut the 1½″ and 2½″ dark red strips that you set aside earlier in half. Each strip should be 11″ or longer after cutting in half.

2 Piece the 1½″ strips of dark red to either side of the 1½″ dark gray strip that you set aside earlier. Subcut into 7 strips 1½″ × 3½″.

3 Piece the 2½″ strips of dark red to either side of the 2½″ dark gray strip that you set aside earlier. Subcut into 4 strips 2½″ × 3½″. **Fig. E**

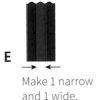

E

Make 1 narrow and 1 wide.

Dark Gray and Black Strips

1 Cut the 1½″ × width of fabric strip of dark gray in half. Piece to either side of the 1½″ × 7″ strip of black. Subcut into 4 strips 1½″ × 3½″.

2 Cut the 2½″ × width of fabric strip of dark gray in half. Piece to either side of the 2½″ × 7″ strip of black. Subcut into 2 strips 2½″ × 6½″. **Fig. F**

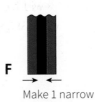

F

Make 1 narrow and 1 wide.

Block Construction

1 Add 2½″ × 6½″ strips of the outer color to each 2½″ × 6½″ strip-pieced unit, to make 6½″ × 6½″ squares.

2 Add 1½″ × 3½″ strips of the outer color to each 1½″ × 3½″ strip-pieced unit, to make 3½″ × 3½″ squares.

Make no large and 28 small.　Make 17 large and 19 small.　Make 9 large and 28 small.　Make 6 large and 14 small.　Make 4 large and 7 small.　Make 2 large and 4 small.

Assemble Small Blocks into Bigger Blocks

1 Sew a solid yellow 3½″ × 3½″ square and 3½″ × 6½″ strip to a yellow 3½″ × 3½″ block.

Make 4.

2 Sew 1 yellow 3½″ × 3½″ block, 2 yellow-orange 3½″ × 3½″ blocks, and 1 solid yellow 3½″ × 3½″ square together.

Make 12.

3 Sew 3 red-orange 3½″ × 3½″ blocks and 1 yellow-orange 3½″ × 3½″ block together.

Make 7.

4 Sew 3 red-orange 3½″ × 3½″ blocks and 1 red 3½″ × 3½″ block together.

Make 2.

5 Sew 3 red 3½″ × 3½″ blocks and 1 red-orange 3½″ × 3½″ block together.

Make 1.

6 Sew 3 red 3½″ × 3½″ blocks and 1 dark red 3½″ × 3½″ block together.

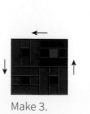

Make 3.

7 Sew 3 dark gray 3½″ × 3½″ blocks and 1 dark red 3½″ × 3½″ block together.

Make 1.

8 Sew 3 dark red 3½″ × 3½″ blocks and 1 dark gray 3½″ × 3½″ block together.

Make 1.

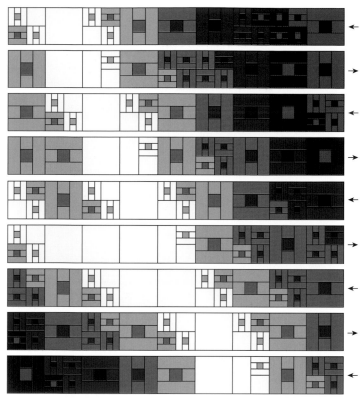

Quilt Assembly

Piece the rows according to the quilt assembly diagram, then sew the rows together to finish the quilt top.

Finishing

Layer, quilt, and bind as desired.

Quilt assembly

The sample was quilted using a flowing pantograph reminiscent of flames. Any single color of thread would have stood out in some area, so I chose variegated thread to help tie the colors in the quilt together.

9

Extending Lines

When thinking about settings for a quilt block, it is worth noting whether or not there are any strong lines running through your block that could be extended across a quilt. Extending existing lines is one of the easiest ways to lead your viewer's eye across the quilt top, which is one of the keys to great design!

Not all blocks will have this feature, but here are some examples. Look for blocks that have features running all the way to the edge, and that, in a traditional layout, are intended to connect to adjoining blocks without sashing in between.

Structured Knot

North Wind

Extending Existing Lines

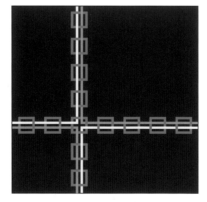

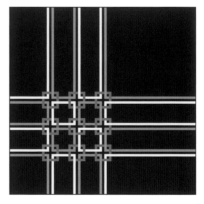

After extending the lines in a block across the quilt, you can add additional elements to the design. Start with the Structured Knot block (above). The orange and yellow lines can extend across the quilt.

For additional interest, you could try adding more aqua squares along the extended lines. Notice also that in this example, the point where the horizontal and vertical lines meet has been moved off center, in accordance with The Rule of Thirds (page 42).

The original block was intended to interlock with adjacent blocks, and it's often nice to preserve that aspect of the traditional pattern when this is the case; so instead of adding aqua squares to the extended lines, you could instead create a larger area of interlocking blocks.

NOTE | *Find the Structured Knot pattern at the end of the chapter (**Buckles**, page 81).*

Keeping the extended lines plain (without added aqua blocks) is a somewhat cleaner look, reminiscent of a neatly wrapped package.

Adding Additional Elements

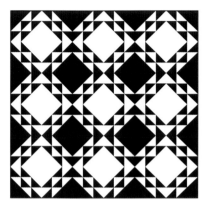

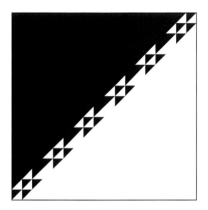

Take a look at the North Wind block (previous page). This block, in a traditional quilt, would typically be set as shown.

However, the block contains a very strong diagonal line, so try setting a single line of blocks across the quilt to see what happens. This has created an interesting diagonal line across the whole quilt, with the triangles appearing to meet at the midpoint.

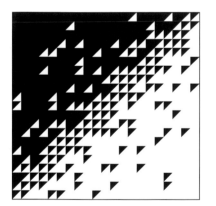

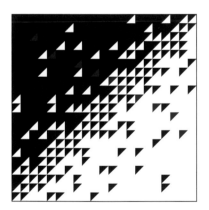

You could emphasize this sense of meeting further by adding more triangles to the quilt. This example includes an element of disintegration, too.

It's always good to consider whether adding an accent color could further improve your design.

This design has created two separate large sections of negative space, illustrating that not all negative space needs to be the same fabric. When there is a clear dividing line, as here, it can be very effective to have multiple areas of negative space in contrasting colors.

Lines That Aren't Lines

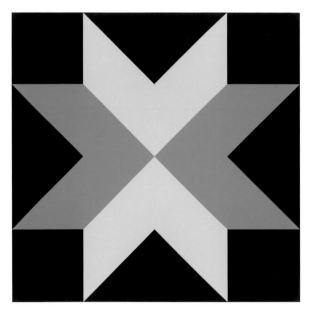

Don't let yourself be limited by the idea of literal lines in your quilt block, though. Any time there is a strong element of direction in a quilt block, it's worth considering how you can use that to your advantage. For example, this star block is made up of chevrons, which function as arrows pointing to the center of the star.

You could expand on this element, and add more arrows pointing to the block. You have still created strong lines in the quilt without including any long straight seams.

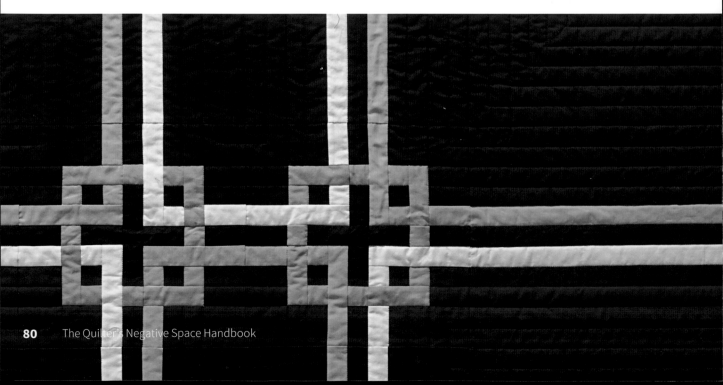

Buckles

The lines in these blocks are extended to create visual motion across the whole quilt. Use a facing to finish the quilt to ensure they don't abruptly end at the edge!

Finished block:
11″ × 11″

Finished quilt:
77″ × 77″

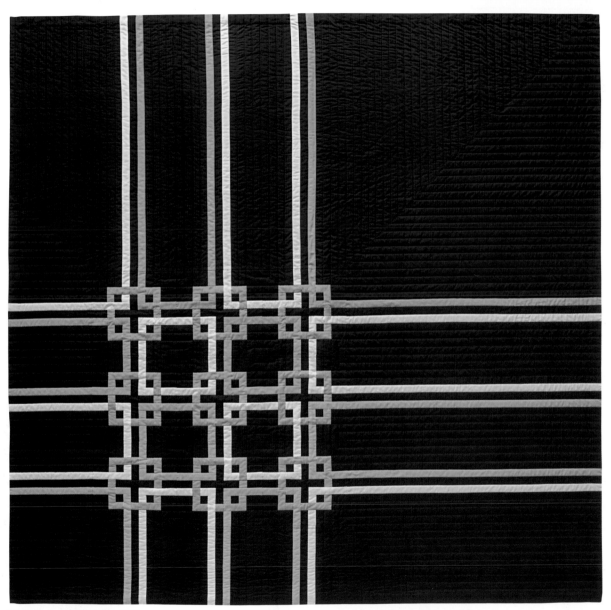

Made by Sylvia Schaefer, 2017

Materials

Dark blue solid:
5 yards for background

Aqua solid:
1/3 yard for blocks

Yellow solid:
3/4 yard for blocks

Orange solid:
3/4 yard for blocks

Batting: 85″ × 85″

Backing: 7 1/8 yards

Facing: 5/8 yard

Cutting

Dark blue solid

- Cut 1 strip 33 1/2″ × width of fabric; subcut into 1 strip 33 1/2″ × 37 1/2″.

- Cut 1 strip 15 1/2″ × width of fabric; subcut into 1 strip 15 1/2″ × 33 1/2″.

- Cut 3 strips 11 1/2″ × width of fabric; subcut into:

  1 strip 11 1/2″ × 37 1/2″

  1 strip 11 1/2″ × 15 1/2″

  4 strips 11 1/2″ × 8 1/2″

  2 strips 11 1/2″ × 4 1/2″

- Cut 4 strips 8 1/2″ × width of fabric; subcut into 4 strips 8 1/2″ × 33 1/2″.

- Cut 4 strips 4 1/2″ × width of fabric, subcut into:

  2 strips 4 1/2″ × 33 1/2″

  36 strips 4 1/2″ × 2 1/2″

- Cut 3 strips 2 1/2″ × width of fabric; subcut into 36 squares 2 1/2″ × 2 1/2″.

- Cut 16 strips 1 1/2″ × width of fabric. Reserve 2 for strip piecing and subcut the remaining strips into:

  6 strips 33 1/2″ × 1 1/2″

  6 strips 11 1/2″ × 1 1/2″

  9 strips 5 1/2″ × 1 1/2″

  54 strips 2 1/2″ × 1 1/2″

Aqua solid

- Cut 7 strips 1 1/2″ × width of fabric. Reserve 2 for strip piecing and subcut the remaining strips into:

  36 squares 1 1/2″ × 1 1/2″

  36 rectangles 3 1/2″ × 1 1/2″

Orange and yellow solids (from each)

- Cut 14 strips 1 1/2″ × width of fabric. Reserve 1 for strip piecing and subcut the remaining strips into:

  6 rectangles 33 1/2″ × 1 1/2″

  6 rectangles 11 1/2″ × 1 1/2″

  18 rectangles 5 1/2″ × 1 1/2″

  18 rectangles 2 1/2″ × 1 1/2″

NOTE | *For tips on cutting and piecing long strips of fabric, see Chapter 11 (page 92).*

Buckle Blocks

1 Using the reserved 1½″ × width of fabric strips, piece an aqua strip and an orange strip to each side of a dark blue strip. Piece an aqua strip and a yellow strip to each side of a second dark blue strip. Press toward the dark blue. Subcut each strip set into 18 strips 3½″ × 1½″. **Fig. A**

2 Sew a 4½″ × 2½″ dark blue rectangle to a 1½″ × 2½″ orange strip. Sew an orange unit from Step 1 to a 3½″ × 1½″ aqua strip; sew this unit to a 2½″ × 2½″ dark blue square. Sew these 2 units to a 5½″ × 1½″ orange strip as shown, pressing as indicated by the arrows. Make 18. Following the quadrant assembly diagram, assemble the orange quadrants. **Fig. B**

3 Repeat Step 2 using yellow strips instead of orange. **Fig. C**

4 Sew 2½″ × 1½″ dark blue strips to opposite sides of a 1½″ × 1½″ aqua square. **Fig. D**

Sew 2½″ × 1½″ dark blue strips to one side of each of 2 aqua 1½″ × 1½″ squares. Sew a 5½″ × 1½″ strip to the opposite side of one of the aqua squares. Sew the other end of the 5½″ strip to the other aqua square to make 1 long strip. **Fig. E**

5 Assemble the block. **Fig. F**

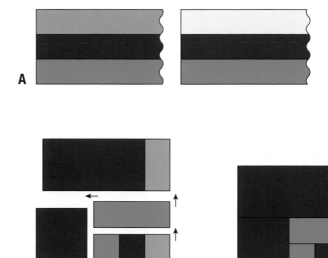

A

B Quadrant assembly. Make 18.

C Make 18.

D Make 18.

E Make 9.

F Make 9.

Panel Assembly

1 Piece the side panels as shown, using 2 dark blue strips 4½″ × 11½″, 3 yellow strips 1½″ × 11½″, 3 orange strips 1½″ × 11½″, and 2 dark blue strips 8½″ × 11½″. Repeat to make a second side panel using strips 33½″ long instead of 11½″ long. **Fig. G**

2 Piece the top and bottom panels as shown, using 1 dark blue strip 15½″ × 11½″, 3 yellow strips 1½″ × 11½″, 3 orange strips 1½″ × 11½″, 2 dark blue strips 8½″ × 11½″, and 1 dark blue strip 37½″ × 11½″. Repeat to make a second panel using strips 33½″ long instead of 11½″ long. Pay careful attention to the placement of the orange and yellow strips. **Fig. H**

Quilt Assembly

1 Following the block assembly diagram, sew the blocks together into a 3 × 3 panel. **Fig. I**

2 Add the side panels to the block panel, as shown in the quilt assembly diagram, matching the orange and yellow strips.

3 Add the top and bottom panels, matching the orange and yellow strips. **Fig. J**

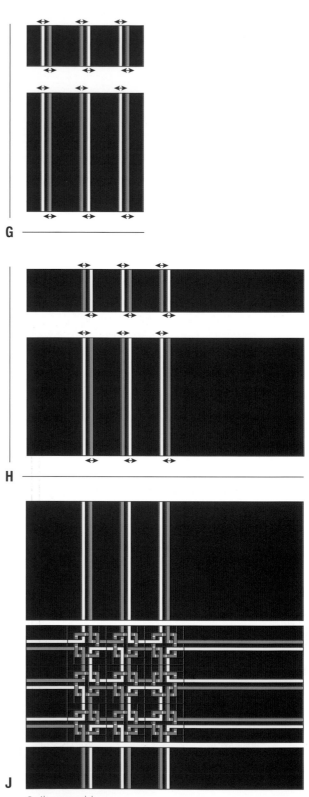

G

H

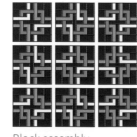

I

Block assembly

J

Quilt assembly

Finishing

1 Layer and quilt as desired.

2 To finish your quilt, cut 6 strips of facing fabric 2½″ × width of fabric. Piece end to end and press in half lengthwise.

3 Cut 2 strips 77½″ (or the actual width of your quilt after quilting) and 2 strips 76½″ long (or about 1″ shorter than the actual length of your quilt after quilting).

4 With raw edges aligned, place the 77½″ strips onto the top and bottom edges of the front of the quilt and pin.

5 With raw edges aligned, center the 76½″ strips along the length of the front sides of the quilt and pin. These strips should overlap the strips placed in Step 4, as shown in the diagram (at right), but should not extend all the way to the corners of the quilt.

6 Stitch around the perimeter of the quilt top ¼″ from the edge, stopping to pivot at corners, as indicated by the dashed line. **Fig. K**

7 Clip the corners of the quilt, clipping the backing and batting very closely to the facing stitching line.

8 Turn the facing toward the back, pressing with a hot iron as needed, and hand stitch it to the back.

K

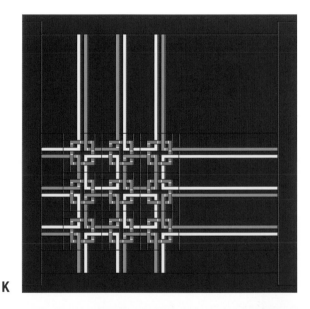

Straight lines echo the overall design of the quilt.

Realizing Your Design

Hopefully, at this point, your head is brimming with ideas for new quilts; perhaps you've even made some sketches already. However, your work has only just begun. You need to choose fabrics, figure out how to actually make the quilt, and then, eventually, quilt it (or at least tell your longarm quilter what you envision). This section aims to give you some food for thought on all these details.

10

Fabric Choices

When you think about a quilt with a lot of negative space, an expanse of solid fabric might come to mind; but solids, while an excellent choice, are far from your only option. The main thing to keep in mind is that the negative space shouldn't overshadow the rest of the design. You want your negative space to add interest to, rather than draw attention away from, your piecing.

Assessing the Design

How do you ensure that your main elements are not overshadowed? Try stepping back a few paces to view your design from a distance. It's even helpful to look away for a minute or two, then look back at the design. If you already have some pieced blocks, put them up on a design wall and step back or take a photo (convert it to black and white for extra insight on how your fabrics work together). Are any fabrics or colors distracting you? Where do your eyes land? Is that the first thing you want the viewer to notice about your quilt?

Choosing Colors

A great design works in many different colors. In some cases, such as *Northern Lights* (page 19) or *Jewel Drop* (page 63), the quilt design may remind you of something that can inspire your colors. Fabric collections usually have a unified color scheme and are a great choice. If you're truly stumped, though, there is plenty of color inspiration to be found online. You can find entire websites dedicated to color schemes (see Resources, page 110), and a search on Pinterest for "color palette" or "color schemes" will bring up thousands of results. There are even websites on which you can upload your own photos and generate a color scheme. Sometimes a color grouping that looks great as a palette doesn't work well for a quilt, so keep playing until you find one that you love.

Color palette generated from a flower photo

Using Prints

Once you have settled on a design and a color scheme, it's time to choose fabric for your negative space. Aside from solids, you could use a print fabric, such as in *Every Which Way* (page 54). Because you don't want to draw attention away from the main elements of your design, it's best to stick with a fabric that isn't overly busy in its colors. As a general rule, stick with prints that use only small accents of another color; tone-on-tone or low-volume prints are a great choice.

Low-volume fabrics

Tone-on-tone fabrics

Piecing the Background

You can also piece the negative space in multiple fabrics. This adds interest to the negative space, but the same guidelines about limiting the color palette in the fabric still apply.

If you like a scrappy look, go ahead and use a different fabric for every piece of the background! Low-volume fabrics are a great choice if you want a light-colored background but don't want to use a solid. *gNOmEL* is an example of a low-volume background.

If you are working with colored fabrics, particularly solids and near-solids, try purchasing several different manufacturers' versions of, for example, a navy solid. You will find that each shade is slightly different, and combining them adds interest to your background without distracting from the design. This is the approach I took for *Main Sequence*.

Continuing Block Elements into the Negative Space

Particularly if you are working with non-square blocks, continuing the block shape into the negative space is a good approach. In *Main Sequence*, the blocks are hexagons, and continuing this piecing into the negative space with an assortment of dark blues adds a great deal of interest.

As discussed in Chapter 6 (page 50), a further extension of this concept is to piece ghost blocks in fabrics close to the background colors.

gNOmEL, pieced by members of Stash Bee, quilted by Sylvia Schaefer, 60″ × 60″, 2017

Main Sequence, pieced by members of Stash Bee, quilted by Sylvia Schaefer, 54″ × 72″, 2014

Detail of *Every Which Way* (page 54). Notice the print background and the piecing within the block.

Gradients

If you place your fabrics more deliberately, you can create a gradient across the negative space. To do so effectively, you will typically want to continue using shapes derived from the blocks, as in *Mountain Rainbows* where the piecing forms a chevron pattern, and those chevrons then continue across the whole quilt.

Another example of a gradient with fabric is *Corona* (page 59), where a simple block of half-square triangles makes up the entire quilt.

Mountain Rainbows, by Sylvia Schaefer, 36˝ × 36˝, 2015

Buying Fabric

The background in a quilt with a lot of negative space typically requires several yards of fabric if you are not going the scrappy route. I try to use my stash for blocks but usually purchase background fabric specifically for a project once I've calculated how much is needed. However, if you prefer to have background fabric on hand, or just stumble across one you love, I recommend buying at least 4 yards so you'll have enough for a decent-sized project.

11 Making the Quilt

Once you have created a quilt design that makes your heart sing, you are still left with the task of figuring out how to actually construct it, and quilts with extensive negative space can present a challenge in this regard. The information in this chapter is intended to help you piece your top.

Avoiding Unnecessary Seams

Most of the quilt designs discussed in this book are still on a grid-based layout; the negative space is, essentially, just missing blocks. It would, therefore, be simplest to cut pieces of background fabric the same size as your missing blocks and piece them all together as you would normally. However, that's a whole lot of unnecessary seams and extra sewing time that you could be using to move on to the next project on your list!

This is the *Northern Lights* project (page 19). The layout involves both blocks and sashing.

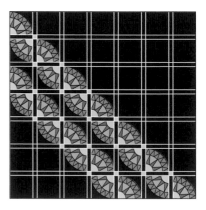

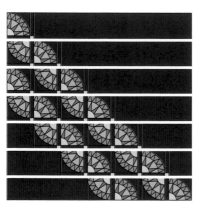

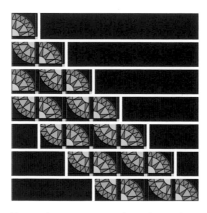

To find the best way to construct this quilt and avoid sewing excess squares and sashings, first find rows (or columns) in which you can sew the quilt together most easily. I prefer to avoid Y-seams unless absolutely necessary.

From there, you can break up the rows further into manageable sections. The bottom row in this case is narrower than the others because it does not include sashing strips, but that's okay!

To calculate the size of the strips in this example, you would add together the *finished* dimensions of the blocks and sashing strips that the larger fabric piece is replacing, then add ½″ for seam allowance.

These same principles apply when replacing portions of a block with negative space, as in the disintegrating Churn Dash block example (page 60) from Chapter 7.

Dealing with Large Pieces of Fabric

Cutting

There are several ways of measuring a long (or extra-wide) strip of fabric when quilting rulers don't come much longer than 24˝.

- For strips shorter than twice the length of your ruler, fold the fabric in half. Be careful to square your first cut to be exactly perpendicular to the fold, or you will end up with a V-shaped strip.

- If you have a cutting mat that is large enough, use the measurements on it. These measurements are designed to be accurate, despite what you may have heard.

- You can use a measuring tape to mark the desired length and cut at the markings. (Double-check the accuracy of your measuring tape with a ruler, though, as old tapes can occasionally become distorted.) Make sure to measure in several places across the fabric to avoid cutting at an angle.

- You can butt up quilting rulers against each other to make up the full length or width. I find this method to be the most accurate. Be sure to double-check your math with a calculator before cutting, however, as it's easy to make an error.

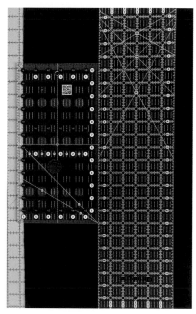

Two quilt rulers butted up against one another to measure a strip wider than the ruler

Piecing

Sewing long seams, and especially long narrow strips, requires special care, as the edges distort easily while sewing and can result in the ends not matching up. These tips will help your quilt top come out nice and square.

- Starch your fabric well before cutting. This minimizes its ability to stretch while sewing.

- While it's tempting to skip pinning, this step is essential when dealing with long seams. Match up the ends of your strips and pin, then fold them in half and pin at the center point. Insert more pins in between as needed, ensuring that the fabric is evenly distributed. This also helps you ease the fabric when the lengths of your strips are a little off.

- If your quilt top is made up of multiple strips, alternate the direction in which you sew them together.

- When strips are extremely narrow, it's best to sew both edges before pressing your seams, as this helps stabilize the strip and prevents distortion from your iron.

Cutting Setting Triangles for Rotated Blocks

To set your block at an angle without wasting too much fabric, you will want to frame your block with triangles as in *Icy Feathered Star* (page 28).

Determine Size of Rectangles

The triangles are formed by cutting rectangles in half along the diagonal, but you will need to do a little math to calculate exactly how big to cut your rectangles. This is where high school trigonometry (that's the study of triangles, if you've blocked out the memory!) finally comes in handy—but never fear, it's easy!

You will need two pieces of information: the *finished length* of your block's edge and the *angle* at which you'd like to rotate it. (Write the numbers with decimals.)

Finished edge: _____

Angle of rotation: _____

To calculate the *finished* edges of the rectangle you will be cutting, use the chart (at right) to look up the sine and the cosine of your angle and multiply them by the *finished* size of your block. *Note: Your numbers will not be in neat ¼˝ increments—that's okay; you will round at the end.*

Width = _____ × _____ = _____
　　　　　Cosine　　Finished
　　　　　of angle　block edge

Height = _____ × _____ = _____
　　　　　Sine　　　Finished
　　　　　of angle　block edge

Now all you have to do is add extra size for seam allowances, again using the chart.

CALCULATING SETTING TRIANGLE SIZES

ANGLE OF ROTATION	RECTANGLE WIDTH		RECTANGLE HEIGHT	
	Cosine of angle	Add to width	Sine of angle	Add to height
5°	0.9962	5.976	0.0872	0.523
10°	0.9848	3.108	0.1736	0.548
15°	0.9659	2.149	0.2588	0.576
20°	0.9397	1.668	0.3420	0.607
25°	0.9063	1.378	0.4226	0.642
30°	0.8660	1.183	0.5000	0.683
35°	0.8192	1.043	0.5736	0.730
40°	0.7660	0.937	0.6428	0.786
45°	0.7071	0.854	0.7071	0.854
50°	0.6428	0.786	0.7660	0.937
55°	0.5736	0.730	0.8192	1.043
60°	0.5000	0.683	0.8660	1.183
65°	0.4226	0.642	0.9063	1.378
70°	0.3420	0.607	0.9397	1.668
75°	0.2588	0.576	0.9659	2.149
80°	0.1736	0.548	0.9848	3.108
85°	0.0872	0.523	0.9962	5.976

After adding, round your size to the nearest ⅛˝.

Exact rectangle size including seam allowance = _____ × _____
　　　　　　　　　　　　　　　　　　Width　　　Height

Rounded to nearest ⅛˝ = _____ × _____
　　　　　　　　　　Width　　　Height

DECIMAL EQUIVALENTS FOR ROUNDING

⅛	¼	⅜	½	⅝	¾	⅞
0.125	0.25	0.375	0.5	0.625	0.75	0.875

Cut Rectangles

You will need 2 rectangles for each square block. (If your block is rectangular, you will need to repeat the calculation above for the other side and cut 2 rectangles of different sizes.) Cut them in half according to the direction in which you would like to rotate your block.

Block rotated clockwise

Block rotated counterclockwise

Cut 2. Cut setting triangles
from top left to bottom right.

Cut 2. Cut setting triangles
from top right to bottom left.

Sew Triangle

When sewing your setting triangles onto the block, align the wider of the two acute (non-right) angles with the corner of your block; it should overhang a very little bit. The sharp point will overhang the edge of your block quite significantly. You can trim this corner after sewing on your triangle.

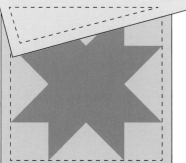

It may help you to mark the corners of the seamlines (shown as dotted lines) on the block and setting triangle, and line those up.

Calculating Yardage

You're ready to buy fabric! But how much will you need?

Yardage for Blocks

Calculating the yardage required for your quilt blocks is relatively straightforward.

STEP	EXAMPLE
1 Determine the unfinished measurements of each piece in the block.	3½″ × 4½″
2 Determine the number of pieces of each size that are needed for the quilt.	18 pieces
3 Divide the width of your fabric by one of the dimensions of the piece to obtain the number of pieces per strip. Round this number down if necessary.	40″ usable fabric width ÷ 3½″ = 11.4, rounded down = 11 pieces per strip
4 Divide the number of pieces needed by the number per strip calculated in Step 3. Round this number up to obtain the number of strips needed.	18 ÷ 11 = 1.6, rounded up = 2 strips
5 Multiply the number of strips needed by the other dimension of your pieces.	2 × 4½″ = 9″
6 Repeat for other pieces cut from the same fabric and add together. Divide by 36″ to obtain a yardage; you should purchase a little extra to account for cutting errors and shrinkage.	9″ ÷ 36″ = ¼ yard

Yardage for Negative Space

Determining the amount of fabric needed for a quilt with a lot of negative space can be challenging, as there are often many pieces with different measurements to keep track of. While the technique described (on the previous page) works, it can be quite wasteful to cut your negative space using a separate strip for each size of piece. I have found that the best way to calculate this yardage is to create a cutting diagram.

You can use graph paper to make such a diagram. Draw a large box 40 cells (for 40″ usable width, with each cell representing 1″) high, then begin drawing in your pieces. After you have drawn all pieces, count the cells in the length and divide by 36″; this is your yardage.

If you are comfortable with computers, you can also use any illustration program that allows you to draw boxes in a specific size (I prefer Adobe Illustrator) to do exactly the same thing. It's easiest to work at actual scale, so zoom way out and create a box 40″ (or the usable width of the fabric you plan to use)

high by 200″ (or whatever you think is far more fabric than you will need). Then begin filling it with boxes the size of your pieces, beginning at the left-hand side. When you have drawn all your pieces, move the right-hand edge to line up with your pieces, and note the final width. Divide by 36″ to get your yardage.

TIP

If your drawing program doesn't allow you to work at full scale, you can certainly draw this diagram at reduced scale, but I always end up making scaling errors and therefore prefer full size.

Whatever technique you use, don't forget to add a little extra at the end so you have enough fabric in case you make any errors. And don't forget to account for your binding, either, if you plan to use the same fabric as the negative space!

You can tape multiple pieces of graph paper together if you are making a large quilt with a lot of negative space.

12 Quilting Choices

You've designed your quilt, chosen your fabrics, pieced your blocks, and now you have a finished quilt top. Hooray—it's time to think about the quilting!

Types of Quilting

Because there are few other design elements in the negative space, it is a place to let your quilting shine. However, that doesn't mean that the quilting you choose has to be complex. The key is to select a quilting design that will tie the negative space into the quilt as a whole. This can be as simple as walking-foot quilting or an allover free-motion design that covers both the pieced blocks and the negative space, or it can be custom or heirloom-style quilting, where different areas of the quilt are quilted with different designs.

Walking-Foot Quilting

Quilting using a walking foot is popular in modern quilting and for good reason. Simple straight lines tie the negative space and blocks together by continuing the quilting design across all areas, and it can provide lovely texture without detracting from the piecing. The lines in the quilting draw the eye from the pieced section to the negative space and back. *Every Which Way* (page 54) uses this style of quilting.

You can add a little more interest to your straight-line quilting by changing direction to follow the general contours of the piecing, as in *Buckles* (page 81). Combining walking-foot quilting in the negative space and free-motion quilting in the blocks can also create an interesting effect, as in *Mountain Rainbows* (page 91).

Detail of *Mountain Rainbows* (page 91)

Kite Block Mini, by Sylvia Schaefer, 20″ × 20″, 2016

An example of spiral quilting on a mini quilt

Another option is to quilt a large spiral (or concentric circles) with a walking foot. This type of quilting contrasts particularly nicely with piecing that involves sharp angles; it guides your eye across the whole quilt without leading it off the edge.

Allover Quilting

An allover free-motion quilting design is another relatively simple and straightforward quilting option. This category encompasses longarm pantographs as well. Choose a design that feels right for the theme of your quilt. *River of Fire* (page 72) was quilted with an edge-to-edge design; because it was inspired by lava, a flame design fit the theme of the quilt better than straight lines would have. Similarly, *Northern Lights* (page 19) was quilted with wavy lines reminiscent of the aurora.

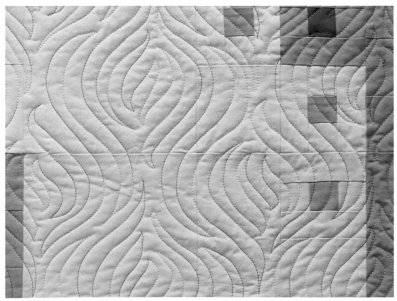

Detail of *River of Fire* (page 72). Notice the variegated thread that helps tie all the colors together. Modern quilters don't tend to use variegated thread very often, but sometimes a quilt just calls for it.

Custom Quilting

Of course, if you love elaborate and extensive quilting, negative space is a perfect place to showcase it. You are limited by only your own imagination, but consider how you can integrate some of the elements and themes of the piecing into the quilting.

Echoing Elements of the Piecing

In quilts that incorporate negative space in between pieced blocks, try echoing block shapes in the quilting. Choosing a relatively dense background fill around these echoed shapes helps them to pop more.

This type of design will typically need to be marked ahead of time. I prefer blue water-soluble pens for light fabrics and a chalk pen or chalk powder for dark fabrics. If the block design is simple, such as an appliqué shape, you can cut it out of card stock and trace around it with a fabric marking pen. For more complex blocks, such as the cranes below, create your own stencil by sewing through a piece of paper with an unthreaded needle to create a perforated block outline. Then, use chalk powder to transfer the design to your quilt top through the holes.

Other elements of the piecing can also inspire your quilting. The blocks in *Jewel Drop* (page 63) create a strong secondary zigzag design, and continuing this into the negative space ties it into the piecing to create a unified whole.

To keep quilting lines straight while stitching some of these types of designs, you may wish to consider using a quilting ruler rather than a walking foot so you don't have to keep turning the quilt every few inches. Rulers have long been popular for use with longarm machines, and domestic machine quilters are beginning to use them as well. When quilting with rulers, make sure you have a ¼″-thick ruler and a specialized ruler foot for your machine; using regular rotary cutting rulers and/or hopping feet could damage your machine.

Detail of *Paper Cranes* (page 45)

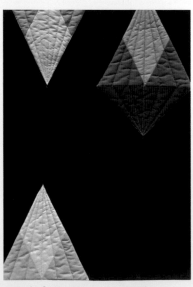

Detail of *Jewel Drop* (page 63)

Some tools for marking quilting lines. I don't recommend heat-erasable pens as the lines can reappear when the quilt is exposed to cold weather.

The Disintegration of the Persistence of Artichokes,
by Sylvia Schaefer, 60″ × 72″, 2015

Theme-Inspired Quilting

You can also choose quilting that reflects the general theme of the quilt. For example, if you are creating a quilt based on the disintegration concept (see Chapter 7, page 58), you may wish to expand on the theme in the quilting by letting elements such as feathers, strings of pearls, or other designs disintegrate also.

Detail of *The Disintegration of the Persistence of Artichokes*

Hand Quilting

Finally, don't forget the potential of hand quilting! All that negative space is a lovely place to let a few hand stitches shine. Choose a thicker thread, like perle cotton, as I did for *Rainbow Sun* (page 38), or even sparkly metallic embroidery floss so that your stitches get the attention they deserve.

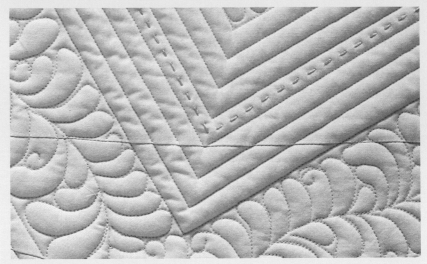

Detail of *Icy Feathered Star* (page 28)

Visualizing Your Quilting

All these possibilities for quilting your quilt can be overwhelming, and if you simply can't decide how best to proceed, it might help to visualize your quilting before you commit. An easy way to do this is to take a photograph of your quilt top, print it out, and draw quilting designs on top.

If you own a tablet, you can save paper and printer ink by downloading an app that allows you to doodle on top of a photo. If possible, pair it with a fine-point stylus to allow you to place your doodles more precisely. (I use the Bamboo Paper app with a Wacom Fineline stylus.)

Testing out quilting ideas for *Icy Feathered Star* (page 28)

Appendix of Piecing Techniques

Paper Piecing

When you need odd shapes and precise piecing in your quilt, paper piecing is the way to go. Begin by making copies of your template. Specialty newsprint-weight foundation piecing paper is easiest to work with, but you can also use plain copy paper.

Cutting Fabrics for Paper Piecing

There are two ways to precut fabrics for paper piecing.

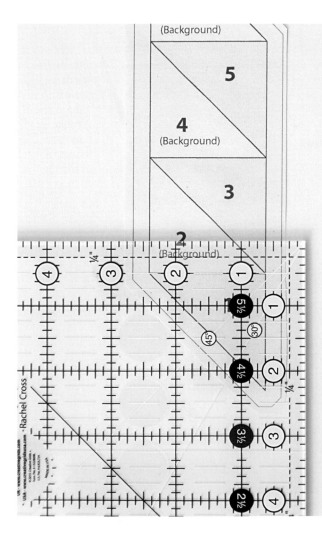

Rectangle Technique

The easiest is to use a ruler to measure the size of the rectangle into which the segment will fit, then add about ¾″ on both sides to account for seam allowance. (If you are new to paper piecing, you may want to add a little extra.) In this instance, a 3″ × 3″ square should be big enough to cover segment 1.

This method is quicker and great for novice paper piecers who need a little extra leeway when learning the technique, but is more wasteful of fabric. Once you are comfortable with paper piecing, you can use the tracing technique.

Tracing Technique

To cut fabrics to approximately the correct size for any given segment, fold the template back along all the seamlines surrounding your segment, then place the template on the *wrong side* of your fabric. Using a pencil or erasable fabric pen, trace around the segment, eyeballing about ⅜″–½″ seam allowance on all sides, then cut out along the marked lines with scissors.

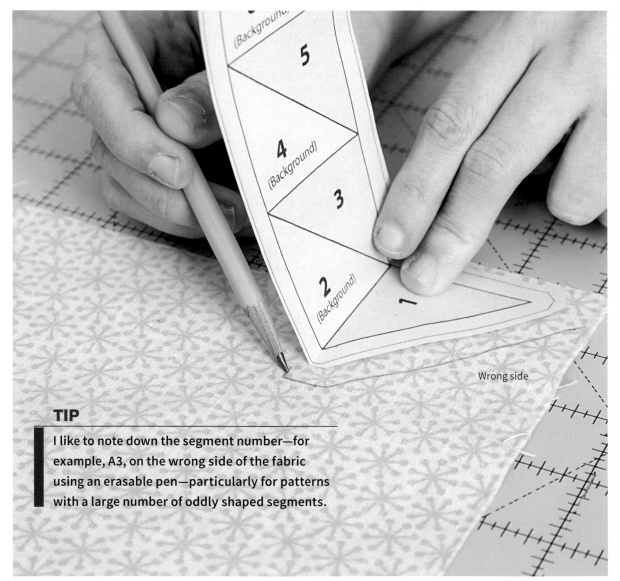

Wrong side

TIP

I like to note down the segment number—for example, A3, on the wrong side of the fabric using an erasable pen—particularly for patterns with a large number of oddly shaped segments.

This method is particularly good for blocks with many odd-shaped pieces.

Piecing Segments

1 Pin a piece of fabric 1 to the back (unprinted) side of the template, with the wrong side facing the template. **Fig. A**

2 Fold the template back on the line between segments 1 and 2. Place fabric 2 with the right side facing fabric 1 so that it covers segment 2 completely and comfortably, with at least ¼″ of excess on all sides. Holding your template up to the light is very helpful in making sure your fabric covers the segment properly. Pin if desired. **Fig. B**

TIP

You can use the edge of an index card, lined up with the seamline, to help you fold the template.

3 Flatten out the template. With a shortened stitch length (I use about 1.7 mm), stitch along the line between segments 1 and 2. Start and end approximately ¼″ beyond the marked line. **Fig. C**

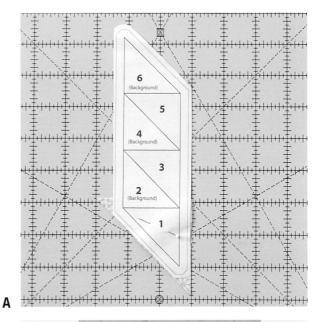

A

B

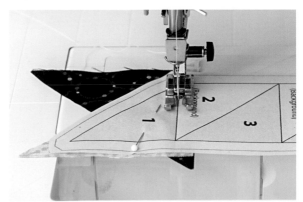

C

4 Double-check that your fabric still covers the segment fully, then fold the template back again and trim the seam allowance to ¼″. A specialty Add-A-Quarter ruler is helpful here, but you can also just line up the ¼″ line on your regular rotary cutting ruler. **Fig. D**

5 Flatten the template again and press the seam. **Fig. E**

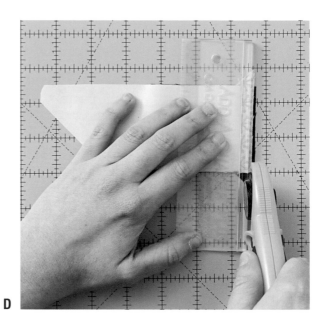

D

E

6   Now fold back the template on the line between segments 2 and 3. You may need to gently pull the template away from the already-sewn seam in the seam allowance. **Fig. F**

7   Repeat Steps 2–6, following the fabric order indicated on your template until you have pieced all segments of the template.

TIP

It's tempting to skip the step of folding back the template, but you will quickly find that, particularly for oddly shaped segments, this step is invaluable for making sure that the fabric actually covers the template completely!

8   Trim the completed piece on the outside lines using a ruler, then gently pull the paper away from the template, using tweezers to help you remove any small stubborn bits of paper. **Fig. G**

TIP

Keep a separate rotary cutter for trimming through fabric and paper together. When replacing your normal blade, move the old one into your paper-piecing cutter.

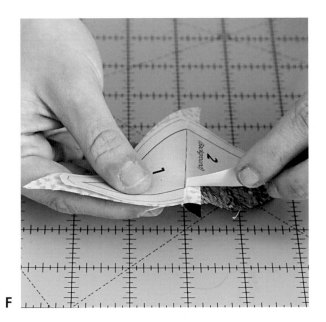

F

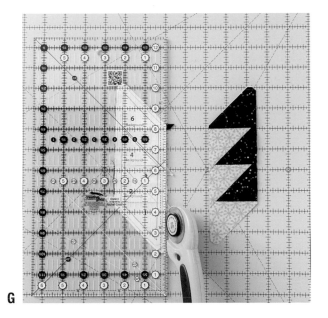

G

Curved Piecing

Adding curved piecing to your repertoire opens up a whole new world of block possibilities.

1 Mark the center point of both your arcs by folding them in half and gently pressing with your iron. With the concave arc on top and right sides together, line up the marked centers and place a pin. **Fig. A**

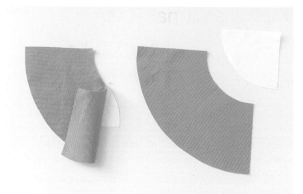

A

2 Line up the 2 sets of edges of the fabrics and place additional pins. **Fig. B**

3 Begin sewing the arcs together, keeping the concave arc on top and using your fingers to adjust the fabrics as necessary so that the edges stay lined up. Remove pins as you reach them. **Fig. C**

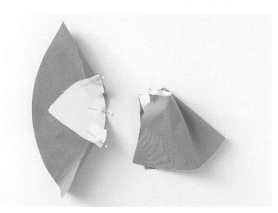

B

TIP

If your sewing machine has a needle stop down function, you will find this useful as you adjust your fabrics while sewing.

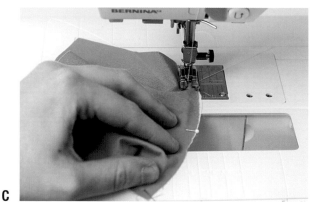

4 Press toward the outer arc, or if the arcs are pieced, in whatever direction the seam falls more easily. **Fig. D**

C

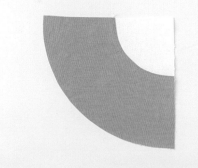

D

Improvisational Piecing

This no-holds-barred technique can be used on its own or to create a new fabric to use in a traditional pattern, such as for the *Rainbow Sun* mini quilt (page 38).

1 Choose 2 scraps of fabric. If the edges of the scraps are not straight, trim one edge of each scrap with a ruler and rotary cutter. Sew the scraps together along a straight edge. (It doesn't matter if the ends don't line up.) Press the seam open or to one side, as you prefer. **Fig. E**

2 Using a ruler and rotary cutter, trim another edge of the 2 scraps. If you started with rectangular scraps, you may want to trim them at an angle. **Fig. F**

3 Add a third scrap along the new straight edge and press. **Fig. G**

4 Continue adding scraps in this manner until you have a piece big enough for your project. You can also sew multiple sections together to avoid having to add increasingly large scraps. **Fig. H**

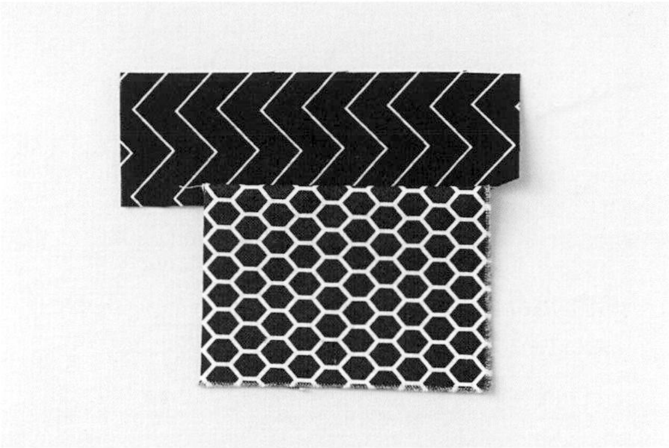

E

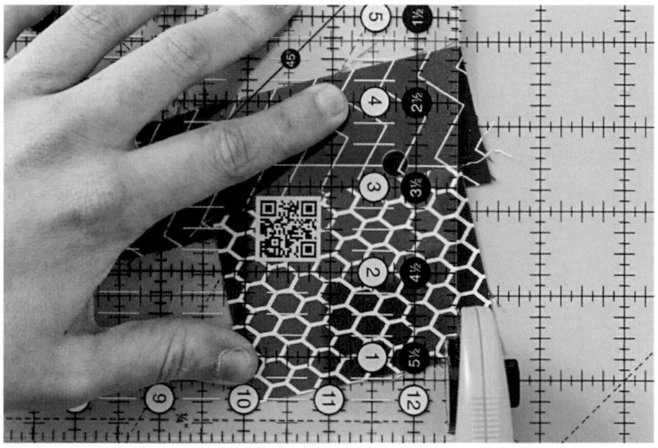

F

G

H

Resources

Quilt Block Collections

Beyer, Jinny. *The Quilter's Album of Patchwork Patterns.* Elmhurst, IL: Breckling Press, 2009.

Goldsworthy, Lynne, and Kerry Green. *500 Quilt Blocks.* South Portland, ME: Sellers Publishing, Inc., 2013.

Papadakis, Brenda Manges. *Dear Jane: The Two Hundred Twenty-Five Patterns from the 1863 Jane A. Stickle Quilt,* Wrights Publishing, 1996.

Pattern Jam: *patternjam.com*

Quiltmaker's 100 Blocks magazine: *quiltmaker.com* > search "100 Blocks" (many volumes to choose from)

Quilt Design Software

Electric Quilt: *electricquilt.com*

Quilt Pro: *quiltpro.com*

Other Quilt Design and Piecing Resources

Collins, Sally. *Drafting for the Creative Quilter.* Lafayette, CA: C&T Publishing, Inc., 2010.

Color Schemes

Design Seeds: *design-seeds.com*
Premade color schemes from inspirational photos

Adobe Kuler: *color.adobe.com*
Generates multiple "color moods" from an uploaded image

Palette Builder 2: *play-crafts.com* > Tools > Palette Builder
Generates matching quilting cotton solids from an uploaded image

About the Author

SYLVIA SCHAEFER is a pattern designer and award-winning quilter. She holds a PhD in marine science, and her background in science often inspires her quilt designs, both directly and indirectly. Her quilts and patterns have been published in magazines both online and in print, and her work has been exhibited and won awards regionally and nationally, including ribbons at Pacific International Quilt Festival, the American Quilter's Society show in Paducah, and MQX, among others. In 2017, she was awarded the second annual Craftsy Quilt Designer Fellowship, allowing her to start her own line of printed patterns sold in quilt shops around the world. She has also appeared on camera in *Fresh Quilting* and *Patchwork Nation*. She lives in Georgia with her husband, Adrian, and their two cockatiels.

Visit Sylvia online and follow on social media!

Blog:
flyingparrotquilts.com

Instagram:
@flyingparrotquilts

Facebook:
/flyingparrotquilts